Praise for Henry Niese and *The Man*

Henry Niese had written a memoir full of
narrative of spirit encounters and an
hair on my arms and brought tears to n
Medicine is a book to treasure.

Luc... ...lair Robson, author of
Ghost Warrior: Lozen of the Apaches

The Man Who Knew the Medicine gives an accurate, insightful, earthy
portrait of the Sioux Medicine Man Bill Eagle Feather. The author affec-
tionately describes how this Sun Dance chief was mentor and guide to
him on his spiritual journey into the Lakota religion. The intertwining
of their lives is gripping, humorous, warm, and inspirational.

William F. Stolzman, author of *The Pipe and Christ*
and *How to Take Part in Lakota Ceremonies*

In this story of the relationship between Lakota Medicine Man Bill
Schweigmann Eagle Feather and artist and healer Henry Niese, both
men come alive. This, humorous, well-written, and powerful narrative
centers around the Lakota concept of what it means to be a relative. By
listening, learning, and trusting in the beyond, as well as in their deep-
est selves, both the author and his teacher Bill Eagle Feather humbly
accept the responsibility of their healing gifts.

Gerald Mohatt, coauthor of
The Price of a Gift: A Lakota Healer's Story

Henry Niese and I have walked through the fields and forest seeking,
enjoying and identifying medicinal plants. My expertise deals primarily
with plants and their medicinal uses. Henry goes beyond that to an idea
of transformational medicine not limited to plants. Whatever it encom-
passes, his way works too, and he covers the subject in an interesting,
readable book. I am a botanist, Henry is more than that, and closer to
the spiritual truths.

James A. Duke, Ph.D., author of *The Green Pharmacy:
Handbook of Medicinal Herbs*

THE MAN
Who Knew the
MEDICINE

The Teachings of
Bill Eagle Feather

HENRY NIESE

Bear & Company
Rochester, Vermont

Bear & Company
One Park Street
Rochester, Vermont 05767
www.InnerTraditions.com

Bear & Company is a division of Inner Traditions International

The incidents that appear in these pages are subjective representations of memories and opinions of the author. In a few cases, the names, descriptions, and
backgrounds of individuals have been altered. The author and publisher accept
no responsibility for historical accuracy.

The artwork that appears on the title page and chapter openers is from a 1976
watercolor by Henry Niese entitled *Heyoka Can Waga* (Clown vision in the
sacred tree). The original piece measures 30 inches by 22 inches.

Library of Congress Cataloging-in-Publication Data
Niese, Henry.
   The man who knew the medicine : the teachings of Bill Eagle Feather /
Henry Niese.
        p. cm.
Includes bibliographical references.
   ISBN 1-879181-98-3
   1. Eagle Feather, William Schweigman, d. 1980. 2. Teton
Indians—Religion. 3. Teton Indians—Medicine. 4. Shamans—South
Dakota—Biography. 5. Niese, Henry. I. Title.
   E99.T34 E346 2002
   299'.7852—dc21
                                2002009192

Printed and bound in the United States at Lake Book Manufacturing, Inc.

10 9 8 7 6 5 4 3 2 1

This book was typeset in Vlejovic with Americana as the display typeface

I wish to dedicate this book to the memory of

William Schweigman Eagle Feather
Henry Crow Dog
Turkey Tayac
Moses Big Crow
Everett Brokenrope
Nida Eagle Elk
Paul George Godfrey
Richard Fool Bull
Rudy Runs Above
Arthur Running Horse
Delores White Hat
Stanley Walking Crow
Maka kin le lecela tehan yunkelo—
Only the Earth endures!

And to my beloved wife and family
And to the *Ikce Wicasa*, the Original People of this
sacred Earth who helped me find my way
Mitakuye oyasin—All my Relations.

*I also wish to thank the many people who have
helped me with this manuscript, including Jane
McGoldrick and Geoff Huck.*

Contents

⊕

It has been said that at the beginning of the Sun Dance, the most sacred of all Lakota rituals, Bill Eagle Feather always raised his eagle wing to the sky and blew his eagle bone whistle and then an Eagle would appear and circle over the Sun Dance ground and disappear into the West.

Richard Erdoes

Preface

In primal times, there was a formal way to treat a child or an adult who had powerful dreams or visions or who heard voices. These things were thought of—and sought after—as gifts from Above. I have experienced these things since childhood and, until twenty years ago, have been too fearful to speak of them.

Nowadays, because of the tyranny of biological psychiatry, these gifts are too often viewed as signs of mental dysfunction. In later life, as I became convinced of their value and reality, I spoke of them. On three occasions, I was taken aside by friends or colleagues who were psychiatrists and was seriously advised to seek professional help.

I began to see the logical structure of these early experiences only when I read *Black Elk Speaks* in the early seventies, when I was about forty-eight years old. John Neihardt, the Nebraska poet, had found Black Elk—the old Oglala Sioux visionary and medicine man—in the early thirties and transcribed the story of his life and visions. I realized for the first time that there was a culture, a body of wisdom, that related to my own experience. Then in the late seventies, my Vision Quest experience and Uncle Bill's teachings helped me to integrate the meaning of those childhood phenomena.

At the end of Neihardt's book, Black Elk mourned the broken hoop, the Sacred Hoop of Indian nations and culture. I promised myself I would do my best to mend that hoop.

With that in mind, my wife, Paula, my son, Cody, and I made an eleven-thousand-mile circle in 1975, camping around the United States and Canada. We met and stayed with elders of many nations—Comanche, Klallem, Crow, Mohawk, and others. Both a Comanche medicine man and a Hopi spiritual leader treated me as though they had expected me to show up and, to my surprise, told me of their vision experiences.

I learned a great deal from these elders, but I was most interested in meeting with Black Elk's folk, the Lakota Sioux.

At Crow Dog's Sun Dance on the Rosebud Reservation, Henry Crow Dog, an old medicine man, began to speak to me of my visions even before I had mentioned them to him, specifically noting the clown, the warrior, and the flute spirits that he said were with me. He squatted down and drew pictures with a stick in the dust. One picture was of the national Capitol building, with the dome hinged back like the lid of a teapot. He made me understand that the elders wanted to impart their wisdom to the U.S. Congress. The Congressmen didn't want to listen, he said; they should listen before it was too late.

With his help, with Bill Eagle Feather's help, and with the help of several other Lakota elders, I came to understand my life, my dreams and visions, and what I should do with them.

This book is about my relationship with C'uwi Wanbli S'un, William Schweigman Eagle Feather, Sun Dance chief and medicine man of the Rosebud Sioux. It is not a biography. It relates some of what he taught me and the ways he went about the teaching. The past twenty-six years of my life have been dedicated to following his instructions and passing on to others what he gave to me.

I want to help.

Amble/Preamble/Ramble

The Bible talks about the street called straight. In my Father's house are many mansions. In my house there are many windows. In the prairie house of an old medicine man who died long ago, the windows and doors are all busted out. The birds fly in and build their houses—in some cases mansions—and the badgers and coyotes wander through.

The street to that man's house isn't straight. There isn't any street, just an overgrown crooked lane two miles from the nearest road. Nobody but the animals goes there anymore.

See, what this medicine man had for an advisor—what the anthros call a "tutelary animal"—was something so powerful that people were scared of it even when he was alive. When he died, nobody would go near his house. The windows and doors got busted out by the range cattle, so the swallows and bowerbirds went in and took over, building their mansions of mud and grass.

The road to my house is far from straight. Sometimes I feel I'm living in a house like the medicine man's old abandoned house—windows and doors busted out, and birds, animals, and people wandering through.

This book is dedicated to the teachers of this way of life, and to Eagle Feather, who opened my windows and doors.

CHAPTER ONE

One More Journey to Make: The End of the Beginning

I was pushing the old pickup too hard, leaning my luck at ninety miles per hour on the interstate. Three-thirty in the morning on September 17, 1980, and no sleep since yesterday, when they'd called me to be a pallbearer for my Uncle Bill Eagle Feather.

It was sixteen hundred miles to South Dakota, to the dry rolling hills of the Rosebud Reservation, home of the Sicangu Lakota *oyate* (nation)—the Brule or Rosebud Sioux in the southwest part of the state. If I was lucky, I'd make it in thirty hours, stopping only for gas and to relieve myself.

I glanced sideways. In the instruments' light I saw the empty coffee thermos and remains of sandwiches and crackers I'd been living on since noon the day before. I shook my head, squeezing my gritty eyes shut for an instant.

When I opened them, there was Uncle Bill staring at me through the windshield. The wrinkled, wise face with its humorous grin and bordering long white braids faded as the pickup's headlights sliced through ground fog covering the highway.

"Hau, Leksi!" ["Hello, Uncle!"]

"So you're riding with me," I thought. "Don't let me do anything stupid. I wanna get there safe."

Sort of a prayer to my Uncle Bill Eagle Feather, medicine man and Sun Dance leader. After the phone call, I had shed bitter tears for a moment. Since then I'd been numb, concentrating everything on making it to the reservation on time.

My Uncle had taught me all I knew about the medicine—the spiritual path. Under Uncle Bill's guidance, I had Sun Danced, Vision Quested, and ceremonied—going for days without food or water to make a sacred relationship with Great Spirit and the Powers of the six directions, seeking power to help the people.

The lights of an interchange flashed by. I was on the alert for state troopers. I scratched my chest, where scars from last summer's Sun Dance were still healing. Feeling around, I located a half-empty pack of gum on the seat beside me.

Late next afternoon I stopped in a rural market in Nebraska just south of the reservation and bought meat, coffee, tobacco, and groceries as the sun was setting. When I got to Joe and Evelyn's place in Two Strike an hour later, the kids crowded around me, happy to see me again. I gave Evelyn the groceries and Joe the tobacco. Evelyn gave me coffee, soup, and bread. Their family was part of Uncle Bill's *tiospaye*—his community.

"You know, I just couldn't go down to Uncle Bill's camp all tired out from the trip," I told Joe. I was afraid I couldn't handle it.

"Well, you're always welcome here," Joe said in his quiet drawl.

Besides being exhausted from the thirty-two hours of driving, I also knew that Joe and Evelyn would be able to give me a good idea of the plans for the funeral.

A few years back Uncle Bill had got the idea that he was going to die. He went up on Tipi Wakan, or Holy Lodge Hill, the hill where he had received his vision, and spent two days digging his own grave.

"That's where I want to go when I die," he had told me. I could envision him, Bill Eagle Feather—who was sixty-something then, and not too strong—sweating and grunting, digging that six-foot hole by himself.

But something mysterious happened, a powerful sign. Convinced he was dying, he went to bed, telling Aunt Hazel, his wife, that the grave was ready. She went up there to check on it herself. The grave was gone, obliterated. A big rainstorm could have washed the rocks and sand back into the hole in that way, but there hadn't been any rain.

Aunt Hazel went back to camp and jubilantly told him what had happened.

"Get up, old man, it's not your time!" she hollered with a big smile.

So he got out of bed, cranked up the old pickup, and he and a couple of the boys went out over the plains and draws to gather firewood and rocks for a thanksgiving Sweat and ceremony. And he had carried on for another three years, teaching, healing, and conducting the sacred ceremonies—*Yuwipi* (a prayer ceremony in which the Medicine Man is bound up like a mummy), *Inipi* or *Initi** (Sweat Lodge), and Sun Dance.

"He was a great man, Grandpa was," Joe spoke reflectively. "And he'll be laid to rest just like he wanted."

Oh yes, the Catholic priests—some of them—were objecting. But Uncle Bill was a traditional, and the medicine men and other traditionals of the tribe were going to make sure he was buried the old way, the way he wanted—no coffin, and

*The words *Initi and Inipi* are used interchangeably. Both refer to the breath of life.

wrapped in his ceremony blanket. His grandson, Chunzila, who had been brought up as a medicine man by his grandfather, was already preparing the ceremony.

Joe said that, in deference to some of Eagle Feather's relatives who had embraced Catholicism, he would be laid out the next evening in Digmann Hall next to the church for one night's viewing and wake. Then he would be placed on a scaffold in the big *tipi* down at his camp, and the traditional ceremonies would begin.

I felt my eyes drooping. I said, "Joe, I'm beat. I got to get me some sleep."

"Well, stretch out on that couch there," Joe gestured with his thumb. "We're ready for bed ourselves."

"*Tunkska!*" ["Nephew!"] The voice was calling me. "Henry! *Hoka hey!* [Come on!] Help me with this!" The tall, heavyset figure of my Uncle Bill stood in front of me holding a big bundle. I opened my eyes. In the predawn darkness of the house, I saw Uncle Bill standing there.

The vision slowly faded as I remembered where I was. I crawled out of my sleeping bag, pulled on my boots and coat, and quietly walked out to my truck. Very carefully, so as not to wake the dogs, I got my Pipe bag and walked away into the vast rolling countryside.

The Morning Star was up, and I walked toward it. After half a mile, I reached the top of a small hill and sat down to await the sunrise. Overhead, the sky was still dark blue and the stars shone. To my left were the Big Dipper and the North Star. In front of me, the sky was turning pale blue and green, and strips of rosy clouds moved along the horizon. The magnificent grassy plains rolled on and on before me, dotted with small clumps of trees marking the hollows and draws.

Two miles ahead, I could make out the draw where the little sandy creek flowed, and the pines, ashes, and scrub oaks that surrounded Uncle Bill's camp. Down in that draw I visualized the log house and the *Inipi,* or Sweat Lodge, and the humble collection of old cars, trucks, *tipis,* and government surplus wall tents where people who wanted to learn from Uncle Bill lived.

People came there asking for healing and counseling, for ceremonies to relieve their grief, or for help in resolving family problems. And people came there to learn the traditional spiritual path, which taught that man was a relative to all mankind, and to the animals, the birds—all living things; to the Earth, the stars, and especially to *Wakantanka*—the Great Mystery, the Creator.

It was there that I had learned to say *Mitakuye oyasin!* [All my relations!] There, I began to understand the relatedness of all things, and the mystery and sacredness of those relationships.

A single beam of pale orange light slowly formed on the eastern horizon, standing vertically over the camp. The sun would be rising in a few minutes, and the camp was directly under the place on the horizon where it would first show itself. No doubt there were a few other people on the hills around the camp, waiting and watching like me. I felt the first puff of morning wind stir my hair.

Stiffly, I got to my feet and, pointing my Pipe to the sky in prayer, I began to sing in a quiet voice the old song that Eagle Feather had taught me.

"Tunkasila, onci malaye." ["Grandfather, have mercy on me . . . I want to live."]

After breakfast, I drove over to the phone booth—the only one in that part of the reservation—and called home to tell my wife, Paula, I was OK.

"Henry, he was here last night," she said.

"Who was there, honey?"

"Uncle Bill! Romie is staying with me and we both heard

him. He was walking all over looking for something. We thought he might be looking for you, so we told him where you were."

"Were you scared?"

"No! We were happy he was thinking of us."

I didn't say anything about my dream or the visit from Uncle Bill before sunrise.

"Look, honey, I'll call again tomorrow and let you know what's happening. They're gonna have a regular wake at the meeting hall tonight. I'll be up all night there."

Somebody was banging on the rickety phone booth door. I turned to see a line waiting for the phone. An old woman with a shawl and fat gray braids, a baby in her arms, was jerking her chin at me, telling me to hurry up.

"Say hello to the kids and everybody. Talk to you tomorrow."

"P'lamiya, Takoja!" ["Thank you, Grandson!"] The old grandma smiled as she squeezed herself and the baby into the booth. *"Was'te, Unci!"* ["My pleasure, Grandmother!"]

I drove south toward Two Strike. After a while I turned off the road and into the open prairie, following the path to the camp. After a mile and a half, I was on the rough part of the lane, down in the draw along the creek. I parked the truck and walked down to the log house.

I saw that Chunzila was putting up the big ceremonial *tipi* with the help of a couple of the boys. The *tipi* was placed directly west of the Sweat Lodge—on a line with the Lodge, the Altar, and the fireplace—about thirty feet to the west.

Chunzila and I shook hands, then embraced without saying anything. Afterward, he said in a barely audible voice, "Grandma and Mom are in the log house. Have some coffee with them."

I could see that he was taking his grandfather's death very hard. Chunzila was only eighteen, but he looked ten years older now. In sadness his face became absolutely impassive and stolid, a mask. It was a large face framed by brown hair, unbraided, hanging over his shoulders and back. He was six-foot-three and weighed about 240 pounds. He was bare to the waist, sweating from wrestling the big lodge poles into position for the *tipi*. The scars from the sacrifice he'd made at the Sun Dance the summer before were still bright red on his hairless chest.

As I entered the log house, I smelled the soup and fry bread cooking. When Chunzila's mother, Delores, saw me she let out a series of cries, the tears pouring down her cheeks. Her face was already red and puffy from crying.

"Oh, Henry, I'm so glad you're here!" She shook my hand and patted me on the shoulder. I shook her hand with both of mine, looking at her wordlessly.

Aunt Hazel turned from the stove with a tin cup of coffee in her hand. On her face was the indomitable look I had seen in her many times before when the going got tough. Deadpan, her lively eyes gone flat, she shook hands and said, "*Wakalapi, Tunkska!*" ["Sit down and drink, Nephew!"]

I took the coffee from her and sat at the old government surplus table. It had been a good table once. It had probably adorned some bureaucrat's office years ago. The chairs, the beds, and everything in this big one-room log house were rickety secondhand furnishings. But they weren't important. Sure, people lived, slept, and ate in here, but the main function of the house was ceremonial. The furniture was always cleared out for ritual purposes, and people sat on blankets on the dirt floor—the old-fashioned way, humbly, close to the Earth—praying for the healing that needed to be done.

As the three of us sipped our coffee Aunt Hazel told me, "We don't want him in no coffin, or even on a hospital stretcher, or nothin' like that. So the boys made him a stretcher—a scaffold out of cedar. He'll lie on that at the meeting house tonight, and then tomorrow they'll bring him down here on it."

Unlike Delores, Aunt Hazel was keeping herself together very well. Delores looked like her dad. She was built big, like him and her son, Chunzila, not at all like her mother, who was small and lively. Delores sat at the table, the tears streaming from her downcast eyes.

In a low voice she lamented, "If only I could have one more day with my Dad, one more hour, just a couple of minutes. Oh, what am I going to do?"

My heart ached and tears came to my eyes. I fought them down. That was the way I felt. Delores was speaking for us all.

Aunt Hazel wiped her face with her apron and said, "Well, he's gone, and he'll never be back. We're the ones who are suffering now and we have to go on. There's lots of work to be done here."

She asked me to help her grandson and the boys take Uncle Bill over to the hall, and then go over to Big Crow's and make sure he had a ride to the hall. The old man couldn't get around by himself.

I went out and helped Chunzila and the boys finish staking down the *tipi*. When we were done, Billy hollered, "*Woyute Was'te walaka!*" ["Let's go eat!"] We went into the log house and filled up on fry bread, soup, and coffee.

By nine that evening, there were a hundred people in the hall, and more coming. Digmann Hall was actually a gymnasium for the parochial school, but it had a large kitchen opening onto the gym suitable for feeding many people. Since the giving and sharing of food was part of all the sacred rites, the place had been the scene of several traditional ceremonies involving the whole tribe.

The scaffold stretcher bearing Uncle Bill was on a large folding table against the long side wall, and folding chairs had been set up to face it. He was wrapped in his old ceremonial blanket, his hands folded on his chest, his braids lying over his shoulders. The whole body was wrapped in a beautiful new rough-woven Indian blanket, with ribbons tying the edges together down his front to his moccasins, as a baby would be tied into a bunting.

At his head and feet were other folding tables bearing flowers and photographs of him and his family. There was a tall tripod bearing his chief's headdress, which had more than a hundred eagle feathers. When he had worn it, the eagle feathers cascaded down his back on trailers that touched the ground. Uncle Bill had been a large and imposing figure when alive, and his dignity and power were still evident even in death.

I sat with Uncle Moses Big Crow in one of the chairs toward the back, near the door. The old full-blood's large frame was uneasy on the swaybacked metal chair.

Big Crow's handsome, rugged face swung toward me and I heard him whisper, "It'll be hard, but I'm gonna stay here all night with him. How 'bout you, Nephew?"

"Uncle, I never even thought about leaving before daylight. I'm with you!"

"Was'te! [Good!]" the old man whispered.

Then he said, "You know, I and Bill grew up together and we were schoolmates, many and many a year ago. In those days, the priests would whip us for speaking Lakota. They dragged us from our homes, cut off our hair—we couldn't even wear moccasins."

I gave him a cigarette and lit it for him.

Big Crow continued, "Nowadays, they're more tolerant. They understand that our religion and theirs—that we're both praying to the same Creator. Some of these priests are even participating in our sacred ceremonies now, Sweat Lodge and all." Big Crow chuckled silently. His sightless eyes behind dark glasses seemed to be scanning the ceiling. "Bill done that. He made them see the light."

The door behind us opened, and an old woman shuffled in,

escorted tenderly by a tough-looking dark-skinned man with long black braids. Mrs. Holy Bear and her grandson squinted and blinked for a moment at the bright gymnasium lights illuminating the scene. Then she resumed her shuffle up the aisle between the rows of metal chairs toward the bundle on the table in front.

Uncle Bill's strong profile, visible from all parts of the hall, was amazingly lifelike. He appeared to be lying on the table taking a snooze. I had seen him lie down like that many times for a few minutes' nap and then jump up, refreshed, to continue the woodcutting, the butchering, or whatever else needed to be done around the camp. For a second I dreamed that he would jump up to greet Mrs. Holy Bear, his old friend's widow.

At that instant, Mrs. Holy Bear began her lamenting, the high keening sound softly piercing my heart. *"EEE-yi-yi-yi!"* she cried over and over again, as she limped toward the body. She touched Eagle Feather's cold hands, bending over his body. Her tears dropping on the blanket, she cried and cried until her grandson gently pulled her away and escorted her to a chair.

I leaned over to Big Crow and whispered, "Uncle, more coffee and cake?" The old man handed me his plastic cup and paper plate. I went to the kitchen and got refills for both of us. After handing the food to Big Crow, I sat for a while, quietly, and then commenced to whisper the story that Paula had told me that morning on the phone.

Big Crow sat silently for a while, then said, *"Ohan!"* ["Yes, it's true!"] For the spirits there's no time or space. They can go anywhere they want in an instant. When he dies, a man's spirit will wander for a few days, looking in on his friends and relatives. That's what happened back at your house."

Around midnight, people began to leave the hall. By three o'clock there were still thirty-five or forty adults and children maintaining the vigil. Most of the little kids and a few of the adults were wrapped in blankets sleeping on the floor. The older boys and girls were out in the parking lot playing, laughing, and talking under the stars in the cool September air. Big Crow still sat, motionless, nodding now and then.

I got up stiffly and stretched, my bones cracking.

"Uncle, I'll be out back of the kitchen. I wanna talk to Uncle Bill's sister."

"You go ahead, Nephew, I'll be here."

I was sitting in the little room back of the kitchen, quietly talking to Mabel and some others who were keeping her company, when someone rapped loudly three times on the door leading outside. I got up and opened the door to let whoever it was in. There was no one there. I looked outside. Seventy-five feet away there was a group of teenagers talking quietly near the main door. No one else was near.

I turned around, the doorknob still in my hand, unsure of whether I had indeed heard the rapping.

"Did you hear that?"

Everyone nodded. I closed the door and went back to my seat.

"Well, you know what they say," Aunt Mabel spoke thoughtfully. "He's probably around, checking up on us!"

A half-hour later, there were two more sharp raps on the door. This time I opened the door wide and said, *"Hau! Wicozanni!"* ["Hello! Good health!"] A faint puff of wind touched my cheek, but no one entered.

Around four-thirty, I was back beside Big Crow, telling the old man that dawn would be coming soon.

A little later I walked outside. Immediately, I was stopped in my tracks by the flaring beauty of *Anpao Wic'ah'pi*—the Morning Star—high in the East, with the rose of dawn coming under it.

Without warning, tears flooded my eyes and I was crying. I saw Uncle Bill before me, stepping through a doorway, as if he had been outside and was coming back inside a house. He said, "Well, Nephew, I have made my prayer. Now it's your turn."

The vision faded. How many times had I met my Uncle like that, coming back into a house before sunrise as I was just going out to make my daily prayer to the Star, as Eagle Feather had taught me to do.

"*Hau, Tunkasila Ksapa.* [Hello, Star of Understanding.] Thanks for this day. Let me do my best today for all my relations."

The owls were hooting in the trees fifty yards away.

"*Wicozanni! Mitakuye oyasin!*" ["Good health, my relations!"]

When I went back inside I smelled bacon. The women were making breakfast, and a line was already forming at the pass-through counter of the kitchen. People were smiling, stretching, greeting one another, feeling good about seeing the night through and enduring the vigil for the sake of this great old medicine man and the family and friends he had left behind.

I stood in line and then brought Uncle Big Crow his breakfast. The old man balanced the heaping limp paper plate full of eggs, bacon, potatoes, and fry bread in the broad palm of one hand, while he forked food into his mouth with the other. It was a pleasure to see a healthy appetite at work.

A little while later, I drove the old man home, and we sat together in Big Crow's humble house, talking while Aunt Nellie made coffee.

Patrick, the thirteen-year-old grandson who lived with them, brought the cups over and gave each of us a big slice of cake.

"You know, nowadays there aren't too many eagles around here," Big Crow said. "When I and Bill were his age," he continued, pointing to his grandson, "there was aplenty of them. But . . . the white ranchers have been killing them off."

He paused. "Well, the day Bill died, a big one swooped down over his camp."

He took off his dark glasses and rubbed his sightless eyes, turned toward me, and smiled.

"They say that eagle came for Bill, just like in the old song—you know," and he began to whisper the words. *"Wanbli gleska wana miye yuha."* ["The eagle has me now."]

It was warm in the old house, sitting in the comfortable worn armchairs by the sheet-metal stove. The old man's head nodded forward and dropped on his chest. It had been a long night.

The eagle crouched on the branch of the low tree, its wings half-open, watching me. I stood across the little creek from it. With a whistling cry, the eagle jumped off the branch and flew at me, its wing brushing my face as it flew by.

I awoke with a start and looked around. Big Crow was still asleep. The fire was almost out. Silently, I stood up and refilled the stove with wood.

For the next two days and nights, Eagle Feather's body lay on its scaffold in the big *tipi* that his grandson and the boys had set up. The scaffold was on the west side of the *tipi*—in the place of honor opposite the door—flanked by the majestic eagle feather headdress on the tall tripod, Eagle Feather's medicine bundle, and his Pipe bag. The medicine bundles and Pipe bags of those who had come from far and near to honor him were there also.

Folding chairs were set up in the *tipi* facing the scaffold. There was a constant flow of mourners in and around the *tipi*. Aunt Hazel, her sad face resolute, gave the visitors coffee in the log house and fed them from large kettles of soup and heaps of fry bread that she, Delores, and the other women friends and relatives had prepared.

In the evening, the mourners went into the Sweat Lodge with Big Crow, Chunzila, and the other men and boys who had been helping out. Sweat Lodge is one of the oldest ceremonies, a rite of purification and renewal. The structure is a small hemispherical dome made of willow saplings, about nine feet in diameter and four feet high. In the old days it was covered with buffalo robes, but since the 1890s blankets and tarps have been used instead. The little dome is thought of as the belly of Mother Earth. We crawl in, humbly, on hands and knees. When we crawl out at the ceremony's end, it is like being reborn, clean and pure.

Inikaga, Inipi, Initi—there are many words for the ceremony. These words imply "breath of life," "life-renewal," or "redemption." *Sweat Lodge* sounds grubby and doesn't carry any of the true meaning of the Native terms. The ceremony can be done simply by itself, but it is fundamental to all others and therefore precedes them—Sun Dance, Vision Quest, singing ceremonies, and others. It may be done once a week or, on special occasions, several times a day.

During the ceremony, rocks are heated in a nearby fire and brought into the Lodge to have water poured over them for steam. In the old days elk antlers were used to handle the rocks, but nowadays they are brought in on a pitchfork.

As the fire keeper brought in the red-hot rocks from the fireplace fifteen feet west of the door, I looked out. Across the flames of the fire pit and through the *tipi's* open door I could see Uncle Bill lying wrapped in his bundle, the rugged profile still expressing the dignity and strength it had carried during his lifetime.

I watched the pile of glowing rocks in the center of the little Sweat Lodge. They were filled with power. All of them carried images—faces, animals, whole scenes. The final stones were placed in the center and the water handed in. Chunzila said, "OK! *Akipo!*" ["Shut it up!"]

The door was closed, sealing off all light from the outside. For a moment we looked at one another, bathed in the red light from the glowing stones. Then, with a crackling hiss, the water was poured on the rocks, and we were engulfed in the searing, purifying blast of steam. Chunzila began to sing, and we all joined in.

"Grandfather, you told us that, from above, you are watching us. Things are difficult. But with your help nothing is impossible in this world. . . ."

At the close of the ceremony, we all cried out, *"Mitakuye oyasin!"* ["All my relations!"] The blankets covering the door were thrown open, and the cool fresh air streamed in over our naked, sweating bodies.

One by one, we crawled out through the low door and stood up, towels wrapped around our waists. As we shook hands and smiled at one another, the steam rose from our bodies into the night. The energy, the refreshment, the feeling of relationship was strong in us all.

We dressed in the shadows behind the Sweat Lodge, and then I escorted Big Crow to the *tipi*, putting my hand on the old man's head as we went through the low opening. Twenty-five people stood or sat inside. Someone was standing by the body and eulogizing Eagle Feather, speaking of the many times he had been helped through the old medicine man's kindness, generosity, and spiritual healing.

He finished with *"Mitakuye oyasin"* and sat down, accompanied by the low-voiced agreement of the crowd: *"Hecetu."* ["It is so."]

A man of about forty got up next. I had never seen him before. He was wearing a suit and tie, unusual dress in camp. His short black hair was parted and brushed back. He had a sharp, intelligent face.

"I am Oglala Lakota from Pine Ridge, Inyan Gliyuwega *tiospaye*—Rockyford community," he began. "I was a warrior,

trained to fight. I was not afraid. The government allowed me
to fly a Phantom jet in Vietnam. All six of my brothers served
in the military and all but one, who was hurt in training, saw
combat. Obviously I was brought up in the way of respecting
the warrior traditions."

He talked about how Eagle Feather had found him a warrior's *wotawe,* or medicine bundle, to keep him safe from harm
while fighting in Vietnam. He told how the bundle had saved
his life. He expressed his gratitude to Uncle Bill's spirit, and to
the family, concluding with "All my relations." He shook hands
with Aunt Hazel and Delores and the other members of the
family and sat down. I later found out his name was Ed McGaa.

Throughout the night the visiting and the testimony to
Uncle Bill's life went on, the fire burning high as the Sweat
Lodge ceremony was repeated over and over. Many people
eulogized C'uwi Wanbli S'un. I knew that if I tried to speak I
would break down in tears, so I kept my silence.

Around four o'clock, exhausted, I crawled into my sleeping
bag and was instantly deep in a dreamless sleep.

The day of the burial dawned gray and drizzly. The rain
continued till ten that morning. As Uncle Bill's bundled body
was brought out of the *tipi* on its scaffold, the rain stopped and
the sun shone intermittently through gray clouds.

Based on sacred tradition and the great honor that was due
Bill Eagle Feather, the plan had been to transport his body to
the burial site on a buckboard pulled by a team of horses.
Unexpected difficulties on his burying day made this impossible, and a hearse was brought in instead. I still look back with
a mind bent on what should have happened. And so, this mod-
ified memory is the account that follows.

The body was placed on the bed of a weathered gray buckboard. A couple of small powerful black horses were hitched to
the wagon. I and three other men had been asked to ride escort

for the wagon, and as the four of us mounted our horses, Chunzila began smudging the body, the wagon, the horses, and all the participants who followed with cedar. He had a big abalone shell filled with smouldering cedar, from which he fanned the smoke with his eagle wing as a purification.

"*Hiyupo!*" ["Let's go!"] The first two horseback escorts were Joe, whom I'd stayed with when I first arrived, and Uncle Bill's son, Isador. They led the wagon out of camp and up the hill, followed by me and John, Aunt Hazel's nephew from Standing Rock, riding abreast behind the buckboard. We wound up the hill, followed by forty walking mourners.

On the flat above the camp was the hallowed Sun Dance site, a circle 150 feet in diameter surrounded by a pine branch arbor. The Sacred Tree, or Sun Pole, stood at the center, still adorned with offerings of tobacco and long streaming cloths, their now faded colors waving in the wind.

The big drum was brought into the circle, and for an hour Eagle Feather, the man who had done so much to revive the Sun Dance religion, rested on his scaffold in the circle while singers and Sun Dancers sang the old ceremonial songs, including the one that brought tears to many eyes, "*Wicasa lawan?*" ["The man I love, when will I see him again?"]

Uncle Bill was the first that I know of to be publicly pierced and to suffer the Sun Dance ordeal in defiance of the U.S. government's ban on all Indian religion. It was for this that he was made Sun Dance chief of the Rosebud people.

The body was returned to the wagon. I and the others mounted our horses, and the long trip began to Eagle Feather's grave on Tipi Wakan, the hill where he had received his vision.

As the wagon with its horseback escort topped the rise near the road, I saw a line of parked cars waiting to join the procession. The wagon was followed out of the camp by twenty cars, as the distance to the burial site was too long for the mourners to walk. I thought of Martin Luther King Jr.'s funeral. They had used a buckboard like this one.

We made our way down the road, the silence broken only by the sounds of the horses' hooves and jingling tack, and the gritty turning of the wagon wheels on the gravel road. Behind us, at a respectful distance, the column of old cars and pickups followed, engines idling, mile after mile.

We began to climb, the grades getting steeper. Looking back, I was amazed to see that the procession was now over a mile long, straggling out almost to the horizon. The cortege was being joined at every lane and crossroad by more and more vehicles. Some of the cars had already broken down and had been pushed to the side by tribal police. The occupants of the disabled vehicles were offered rides in other cars and trucks. Some walked on the side of the road.

At last we turned off the road onto the rolling plains at the foot of the steep hill where Uncle Bill had fasted for so many years before the vision came to him.

"Ho! Everybody walks from here except for the old ones," Chunzila commanded.

The mounted escort and the wagon continued across the plain for two hundred yards or so and then stopped, waiting for all the vehicles to park and the people to form a line of march. Tribal police were organizing the plain into a gigantic parking lot, row upon row of cars and trucks side by side, forming long snaky lines across the prairie. Those in the back of the procession had already parked their cars farther back on the side of the road. I could see them walking the distance toward the old buckboard to join the ranks forming behind the horses.

Chunzila asked the tribal police to allow about thirty cars bearing the old, the sick, and the crippled to drive as far as they could to the base of the hill. Now, the wagon and the horsebacks with all the people following began the final quarter-mile to the hill. As we moved onward, we were flanked on both sides by the proceeding cars, old folks peering through windshields, shawled grandmothers wiping their eyes with handkerchiefs.

When it was too steep to go farther, we dismounted. Chunzila brought the pallbearers together. Since Eagle Feather weighed 250 pounds, and the scaffold was heavy, four of the strongest men were selected to bear this burden to its final resting place. Others would spell these four from time to time.

"My relatives," Chunzila spoke. "It's going to be hard. We're going straight up. We will rest four times. There are plenty of people to help us. *Wana, hoka hey!* [Now, let's go!]"

The four pallbearers shouldered the scaffold. They began the climb. Hundreds of people were climbing with them, the young and energetic already out front above them, leading the way. Four men had been selected to carry the eight-foot-tall staffs, each with one of the sacred colors. Ed McGaa, out of his business suit and dressed in his old Marine aviation combat jacket, carried the red flag, a cloth offering. The footing became difficult, with outcroppings of sandy rock and clumps of prickly pear. The men carrying Uncle Bill sweated and grunted. The hill was already as steep as a flight of stairs. The two in front bent over, carrying their end of the scaffold at knee-height while the men in back still had their end shoulder-high in order to keep the scaffold level.

They rested, others holding the scaffold while the pallbearers caught their breath. I turned to look down the hill and was astounded at the spectacle of hundreds of cars and people darkening the plain below, the hillside swarming with those making the climb to the grave.

Overhead, the cloud cover was breaking up; meadowlarks and doves were flying. On the plain to the east, patches of sunlight moved across rolling grassy countryside. It was becoming a fine day.

When we finally reached the grave, the men at the back were holding the scaffold over their heads in order to keep the body level, so steep was the hill. Many were helping, some holding up the scaffold, others holding onto and steadying the pallbearers.

For me there was a flash of déjà vu—where had I seen this before? Suddenly I realized it reminded me of the great archetypal photograph of the flag raising on Iwo Jima. The marines in that photograph, some bent over at the foot of the the pole and some stretching to lift the top of the pole, were duplicated in the mourners' stances.

Songs were sung, the final words were said. Slowly and gently Eagle Feather's body began the descent into the grave. Aunt Hazel, Delores, and other elder women who had managed to make the climb up the cactus-ridden, rattlesnake-infested hill, sat by the grave, their keen lamentations filling the September air. I looked at the men. Like me, they tried to hold back tears. This was the journey Uncle Bill had referred to so often in his teaching when he said, "We have but one more journey to make."

The eight-foot staffs were placed down in the corners of the grave, each flying a flag of the holy colors—black, red, yellow, and white—as they are offered to the four directions in all the sacred ceremonies. The staffs protruded above ground level about two feet, their colored cloths blowing in the wind.

Four shovels were produced. Chunzila ceremonially dropped four handfuls of earth into the grave.

"O Grandfather, you told me that when we were through with this life our Grandmother the Earth would take us back. It is as you said. *O Maka, Unci. Mi Ina.* [O Earth, my Grandmother and Mother.] Here he is. Take care of him now!"

The pallbearers began to shovel the earth into the grave, sweating, breathing hard. Four others took their places, shoveling continuously. The grave slowly filled up. The women sat upon the rocky ground by the grave, weeping, their shawls and arms about one another, looking like the women in Delacroix's painting *Massacre at Chios*.

Delores was hysterical in her grief, sobbing over and over, "Oh Daddy, what am I going to do? Please don't leave me!" Her large figure was shaking with sorrow.

The grave was filled and smoothed over, the long flags of trade cloth and their short masts draped by the wind over the raw earth. Chunzila stood up and said, "Behold, my relations, it is done. You have seen how my grandfather lived, doing his best in the traditional way, the old way. Now you see he is buried the way he lived."

As he turned away from the grave, Chunzila's face convulsed, and in a sobbing, cracked voice he croaked, *"Ho, hecetu welo!* [So be it!]" And he started down the hill.

I stood by the grave, watching the crowd move downhill, watching cars and trucks pulling out into the road, heading for the traditional feast and Giveaway. I knew the family would donate most of their belongings to whoever would take them as a sign of how poverty-stricken their loss made them feel, and in appreciation for the help they had received in this time of grief.

Far below me, the plains and hills rolled away to the south and east, covered with tan grass and gray sage, dotted with clumps of dark green pines and cottonwoods. Meadowlarks scattered as a big red-tailed hawk came soaring over the hill on the wind.

I thought of the years my Uncle had stood in this place, each time four days without food or water, asking, begging, and finally sobbing and crying for help—a vision or a dream. Days and days of fasting and suffering for the vision that would give him wisdom to help his people. After seven years, when he had been ready to quit and admit defeat, the Spirit had come to him.

I gazed around the horizon, the rim of the world that encircled me. I thought of the Sun Dance circle and the Sweat Lodge—how they were a reflection of this big circle that surrounded me. I remembered listening to Eagle Feather talk about his vision. Now my Uncle was speaking to me again, in the soft, gentle, almost whispering reflective voice he used when he was teaching.

"The Sacred Hoop is *not* broken, as Black Elk said it was. It's all still here! In my vision I went there, and it was beautiful. Bee-yu-tiful! So green. The sun was shining, all the animals and birds were so happy. And I was happy! And I thought, 'Boy! Now I'm safe from harm. No more sickness, no more suffering, no more weariness from working so hard.' It was perfect in every way.

"And then! I received the message! I was to be custodian of this holy place. My work and suffering wasn't over, it was just beginning. And that's the great teaching that I received! That we are all custodians of the Sacred Hoop, the circle of life. We are all custodians of this beautiful mysterious Earth and all that's on it and in it.

"And we all think that there's so much time, that we have a lot of time. But we're only here a short time! Such a short time! We are passin' through here—only once! And we have but one more journey to make."

He had told me this many times while he was alive. I can still hear his voice as I write these words.

The voice faded and I was aware I was alone, the tears running down my face. Beside the grave there was a little stone with a familiar face on it. It looked like him. I picked it up, stared at it a while, then put it in my pocket and started down the hill to where my horse was tethered, waiting for me.

At the Ready As You Ramble

When we hunted, my father would tell me, "Keep that gun at the ready, don't carry it like a damn suitcase!" Jumping quail, rabbit, or pheasant, I learned I had a better chance at a shot if I did what he said.

I also found out in my life that the chances come jumping, buzzing, flailing like game at you, and if you're not ready you don't have a shot. Some opportunities fly by so fast, you've got to give them a big lead to connect, like a pass on a mallard.

You have to be ready to jump, take the big chance. Fear and timid action don't cut it.

Beginnings have never been difficult for me. I jump right in with both feet, sometimes not even knowing what I'm getting into. Some folks have to study the thing from every angle, thinking so much they forget their feelings.

I've seen a lot of people so paralyzed by thought and the need to prepare that they wind up missing the boat completely; they never get started. One guy I know prepared so long for his training that his medicine man uncle died before the guy was ready to accept his teachings.

Not that I don't think about things. I've been paralyzed by thinking too much. But I rely on my instinct and feelings a lot. Whether it's fate or the fact the spirits have been watching over me, I usually come out all right. Let's call it luck.

CHAPTER TWO

Luck: The Chosen One

It was my good luck that landed me in one particular Sweat Lodge ceremony one evening at a 1975 Sun Dance on the Rosebud Sioux Reservation in South Dakota. On our great swing around the North American continent, Paula and I and Cody, our four-year-old son, had left the Crow reservation in Montana a couple of days before and headed to Crow Dog's Paradise to help with his Sun Dance.

Five Sweat Lodges were filled with dancers. The sixth had room for one more. There were ten or twelve dancers in the Lodge, too tired and dry from the day's dancing to say anything much, and I, the stranger who wasn't there to dance. We were waiting for someone—a medicine man—to come and begin the ceremony.

A large, older man with long gray hair in a ponytail crawled into our Lodge or *Initi* saying the customary *"Mitakuye oyasin."* He sat next to the doorway in the place where the one who conducts the ceremony traditionally sits. The doorkeeper began bringing in the red-hot stones, and one of the dancers began to arrange them in the rock pit, the first stone positioned in the West, succeeding stones going to the North, East, South, and the center. He used the traditional elk antlers to move the stones.

The medicine man said, "Too bad! They forgot to give us the herbs." He was referring to *Hante Blaska*, a special cedar placed on the rocks as incense.

I spoke up. "Uncle, I have some herbs."

"Well, put 'em on, Nephew!"

These were the first words spoken between me and Bill Schweigman Eagle Feather, Sun Dance chief and medicine man of the Rosebud Lakota Sioux. I didn't know it then, but it was the beginning of the most important relationship of my life, outside of those with my immediate family. I wouldn't even know his name for another year. Our relationship would last for five years, until Uncle Bill's death on September 15, 1980. He was a master teacher, and for the last years of his life I would become his dedicated disciple.

He was "Uncle" and I was "Nephew" from the beginning. These relationship signifiers are used by Indians and others not only as a sign of respect, but as an acknowledgment of connection. When we were kids, my brother and I were instructed by our folks to call friends of the family "Uncle," they addressed us as "Nephew."

As I placed the herbs on each glowing stone and their sweet odor drifted through the little domed *Initi*, I saw that this big gray-haired medicine man was staring at me with a piercing look. At first I thought that I was doing something wrong, but he said nothing. I later got used to Uncle Bill's fixing me and others with his lancelike gaze. It was his way of seeing beyond the surface appearance of things. I realize now that this beginning contact between us was when he first "saw" me as a prospect. Later in our relationship, I understood that he was always on the lookout for people open to his teachings.

Just before that Sweat, I had the opportunity to participate in another ceremony, *ceh'pi waonye*—the flesh offering. They say that you can't give anything to *Wakantanka,* or Great Spirit, because he owns everything. It's pointless to offer a horse, or any property. But as a token of your good intentions you can offer small pieces of your own flesh as a sacrifice. I wanted to show the Creator that my intentions were good, so I lined up with others when the dance leaders announced they would be taking flesh.

I was scared. I'd never done it before. "How big a piece do they take?" I wondered. When they asked me how many, I said, "Four." Using a needle, one of the dance leaders raised up the flesh of my upper arm and sliced four pieces off with a Gillette double-edged razor blade. Then he spat on the wounds and rubbed a handful of dust on them, stopping the bleeding. I was relieved it didn't hurt too much.

Descriptions of the Sun Dance are available in many books. Richard Erdoes, Thomas Mails, and Archie Fire Lame Deer are a few of the modern authors who have written on this topic. The meaning of the ceremony is so profound I have a hard time answering those who ask about it. Mainly I tell them it's a way of paying our dues to the Great Spirit, but it goes a lot deeper than that. It's a way of giving thanks for many blessings and healings, for the fertility of the whole Creation, and more. Desperate times in war and peace will evoke a prayer or vow, "If you let me survive this, I promise to Sun Dance four days," or, "If you let my mother [or any relative] live, I vow to dance four days."

So the men (and, today, a few women) dance and fast for four days from before sunup to sundown, or thereabouts. No fancy stuff, just standing, enduring, picking 'em up and putting 'em down, left-right, left-right, hour after hour, keeping time with the drum and singers, staring at the Sun. Sun Dance songs are prayers: "Grandfather pity me. I do this so my people will live," and the like. Every hour or two, even five at the most, the dancers get a break during which they can sit in the shade for a while. Then the next round begins, and they repeat the same steps, consecutively facing West, North, East, South. Or they dance in a big circle facing the Sacred Tree in the center of the arbor—the Mystery Hoop—which usually spans 80 to 150 feet in diameter.

Two days later, the Sun Dance was over. The dancers were led out of the Sacred Hoop and given their first food and water in four days. Families ate, visited, and relaxed all over the area, happy to be reunited with their dancer relatives who had fulfilled their pledges to dance that year.

I heard the camp announcer call for those who wished to vow to dance the following year.

"Hocoka hiyupo! [Come to the center!]," he invited. "If you wanna make this sacred vow to dance, enter the Circle and stand in a row on the south side. Don't forget to take off your shoes and moc'sins. This is sacred ground you'll be steppin' on!"

By ones and twos, young men and a few women began to drift toward the dance arbor.

It had been my dream or vision for several years to offer myself in this way. But until now I had not thought it was possible, since it was a Plains ceremony and I was from the East. But I headed over to the south side of the arbor. When I got there, I saw that the *Eyapaha*—the announcer—was the gray-haired medicine man.

I went up to him and said hesitantly, "Uncle, I'm a stranger here, and not sure if I would be welcome out there in the center. But that's my dream."

Instantly, he said, "Take off your shoes!" When I had done so, he commanded, "Now, git out there and take your place!"

As I left him I heard him say, *"Wowas'te!"* ["Good!"]

I stood there with about fifty others, my first time in the *Cangleska Wakan*—the Sacred Hoop or Circle. The others seemed so relaxed, making small talk in low voices. My heart was pounding. I was sweating, trembling. I heard the medicine man saying over the public-address system, "People, behold them. They have taken their sacred vow."

He said it first in Lakota, then in English. About four or five hundred onlookers were standing in the arbor, outside the sacred area, staring at us. I saw my wife, Paula. On her face was a look of astonishment. Seeing me out there was the first she knew of my intentions.

Later, at our campsite, Paula rebuked me, asking why I hadn't told her I was going to vow. "How come I'm always the last to know?"

Apologetically, I explained that I hadn't even known myself until I did it.

What I didn't know was a lot. I was fifty years old, a graduate of the Cooper Union and Columbia University in New York, and an Associate Professor of Art at the University of Maryland. My real education was just beginning.

When we got back home to Maryland, I went to see Turkey Tayac, the medicine man of the Piscataway tribe in Maryland who had been teaching me about roots, herbs, and other things. I had met him a few years before. We got on so well that he'd adopted me and given me a Piscataway name, Go-yom-ac, or Wild Goose. The adoption ceremony was done on the old Piscataway burial ground on the Potomac across from Mount Vernon.

During the wandering stage of his development, before World War I, Turkey had traveled all over the United States visiting other Indian nations. He had spent time with the Sioux and had even picked beets in Nebraska in 1916 with Matthew King and Frank Fools Crow, two Oglala Sioux from Pine Ridge who later in life became famous spiritual leaders.

Turkey and I were walking through the fields looking for plants when I told him of the vow I had made. I figured he'd be sympathetic since he knew about the Sioux religion. His eyebrows shot up.

"What! What in 'nation made you do such a thing? We never did that 'round here! Well, Wild Goose, I got to hand it to you. You got yourself in it with both feet, didn't you?"

I asked him if he'd help me to prepare for the ordeal. He stared at me with a sharpness not unlike that of the gray-haired man out West.

"Well-ll, all right. Start right now! First thing you do is th'ow that away," and he pointed to the cigarette I had just lit. I tossed it to my feet and stepped on it.

"Next—take the pack out your pocket an' th'ow it away!" Smiling, I took the new pack of Camels out of my pocket and sailed it out into the field.

"Now, Wild Goose, don't you let me catch you with one of them things agin!"

He proceeded with his instructions. "You get yourself a couple of jugs. Take 'em down to Lexington Market in Balmer"—his way of saying *Baltimore*—"and get you a couple gallons of fish brine—you know, the stuff they pack the herrings in. You need to get your feet tough for this job. Soak 'em in that brine ever' now and then."

Old Turkey was really practical, I thought. We were walking near my place through a field of corn stubble, the sharp, stumpy six-inch stalks cracking under my boots and catching the cuffs of my jeans. The next thing Turkey said made the skin on my back crawl. He wanted me to run through the field barefoot.

"Don't you think 'bout it too much, just start runnin'. Not now, but when you're ready. That'll really toughen you up good!"

I'm one of the types who walk like a cripple without shoes on, a real tenderfoot. I give myself a lot of credit for following Turkey's instructions. That fall and winter, about once a week, I would walk out of the house barefooted, cross the lane, climb the fence, and stand for a moment concentrating myself on the edge of the field of corn stubble. I would often say a prayer to myself. Most of the time I would say, "What the hell, give it a shot!" and take off running full tilt into the field. It was all a matter of attitude, mind, and will, I found out. Turkey was right. If I thought even for a second about what I was doing, the pain was unbearable.

I would run as hard as I could about a quarter-mile to the top of the hill. There, I would catch my breath and take in the surrounding beauty of the country, never looking at my feet. Then, with a shout, I would rush down the hill to my starting point, walk into the house, and only then assess the damage to my feet. The soles and ankles were always covered with cuts and bruises. I'd let them heal a week and then do it again.

After a month, I could walk on the gravel lane without flinching. And I didn't have another cigarette until the Sun Dance when, surrounded by a hundred dancers, most of whom smoked and who constantly offered their smokes, I had my first in a year.

In June 1976, a week before the ceremonial event was due to begin, I arrived with Paula and Cody, now five years old, at the Sun Dance. We set up our camp west of the dance arbor, near the sequestered area the dancers would occupy the following week. The family of one of the dancers I knew set up their tents in back of ours.

That evening, the dancer, named Loren, came over to our camp. We were talking over a cup of coffee when I saw the gray-haired medicine man walking toward us. "What's this old guy's name?" I whispered to Loren.

He whispered back, "That's Bill Schweigman. He's the Sun Dance chief here." Standing up, I welcomed him to our camp-site and offered him a cup of coffee. After introductions, Uncle Bill gingerly lowered his 250 pounds onto one of the plastic milk crates we were using as camp stools.

"*Ohan!* So you made it back here an' you're gonna dance. You all ready? I see you got your skirt."

He nodded toward the ribboned red and blue ankle-length skirt that Diane Crow Dog had made for me. It was hanging on the tent.

"How 'bout your flesh pins?"

Seeing my blank look he said, "If you're gonna pierce you'll need two. Get 'em off that chokecherry by the creek."

Changing direction, he asked, "D'you bring any more of them herbs this time? We can use 'em in the Sweat." He put down his cup and got ready to move on.

As he stood up, he said, "See that big guy over there? That's Oray, my helper." He indicated a barrel-chested young man about twenty-five years old standing by the dancers' *tipi*. His chest already had many scars from previous Sun Dances.

"Talk to him tomorrow. He'll help you with the pins. Thanks for the coffee." He walked away, shaking hands and nodding to the people in surrounding camps.

The next day Oray helped me find and shape two pencil-sized cherrywood sticks, sharpened like pencils on one end. Uncle Bill, the Dance leader, would use these on me toward the end of the dance, piercing my chest in the most difficult part of the ceremony. Oray was Uncle Bill's apprentice, a quiet man with a funny sense of humor and a beautiful smile. He was from Standing Rock. From the beginning, he was a true friend who helped me over the difficult days ahead.

Of all the many Sun Dances I have danced in, the first was by far the hardest. The difficulty was due in part to my igno-rance. The medicine men always talk about *tawacin,* or *wacin,* which could be translated as "mind" or "will" or "purpose." Mine was imperfectly developed, so I suffered greatly. Instead of keeping my mind and will centered on why I was in that sacred arena, I dwelt at length on my great thirst and my pain.

No one can undergo the rigors of the Sun Dance—four days

and nights without food or water, dancing from sunup to evening, and the sacrifice of the flesh—without a perfectly concentrated mind and will. The true meaning of "mind over matter" began to come clear to me only after my second dance.

That first Sun Dance was also made difficult by the great antagonism expressed toward me by a number of the younger dancers. I was an outsider from the East and a mixed blood, more white than Indian. The elders welcomed and accepted me, and stood up for me. In spite of this support, the week before the Sun Dance was filled with tension as these young dancers tried to force me not to dance. My life and the lives of my wife and son were threatened twice in this period, never directly; they always sent a messenger.

The day before the dance began I went to Uncle Bill Eagle Feather, the dance leader. I was emotionally ragged out.

"Uncle," I said, "these guys don't want me to dance, but I made a sacred vow, and I've been working on it for a year. If I can fill this vow on the hilltop, fasting the four days there, I'm willing to do that."

Uncle Bill looked at me. "If you don't dance, you know what happens? I have to do it for you. Me. You don't wanna put an old man through that, do you? You're gonna dance!"

This was Wednesday afternoon. That evening, I had my last food and drink until the following Sunday afternoon.

Today, having participated in many Sun Dances, thinking back on what I did during those four days, I would have to give myself a D. I had prepared both physically and spiritually for a year. Still, because of my imperfect mind and will, I suffered a lot. I passed out briefly twice. Norman, a young Navajo, had to help me break loose from the Sacred Tree, even though Uncle Bill had pierced me lightly. Today, I would have nothing but pity and scorn for someone behaving as I did.

When it was my turn to pierce, the leaders took me to the

Sacred Tree, or Sun Pole, in the center and told me to pray. Then they laid me down on a buffalo robe. I wore a sage crown, which they took off and put between my teeth, telling me to bite on it to help the pain. My chest was scrubbed with sage. Two of the leaders grabbed a pinch of flesh over my heart and stuck a knife through. Then the flesh pin, well greased with lard, was slid into the wound. The same was repeated on the right side of my chest. I was chewing the sage headband to bits. It hurt so bad I couldn't breathe.

The leaders stood me up, put the crown back on my head, and tied a rope yoke to the pins. The end was in the form of a Y, the two arms of the Y attached to each side of my chest. Then this yoke was attached to a longer rope and that rope's other end was tied to the Sacred Tree.* They took me to the end of my rope fifty feet from the Tree and commanded me to pull hard.

I did not have the will to overcome the pain of pulling the rope taut, so a sag remained in my rope. In later Sun Dances I was able to make the rope as tight as a fiddle string, to the point where it vibrated when it was hit with a stick or eagle wing fan.

Finally, they took me back to the Tree. I prayed there four times then ran backward as hard as I could to break free. The Tree picked me up and threw me down without releasing me. As often as I repeated the process, the Tree would not let me go. In a panic, I thought I would never be free. Finally, Norman grabbed me from behind and fell backward with me. With a snap our combined weights freed me—or so I thought.

Trembling, I turned to shake Norman's hand. He said, matter of factly, "You only broke one side. The rope broke on the one over your heart. Go get another rope."

---

*The rope that ties a dancer to the tree is sometimes referred to as *c'ekpa* (navel cord), binding the dancer to the Tree, to Earth, and ultimately to the Great Mystery—God Almighty. Breaking free has implications of birth and rebirth and is part of the path to enlightenment.

I went back to the Tree and they hooked me up again. When I ran backward, Norman grabbed me again and I was finally free.

I couldn't figure out how a little piece of my flesh had been able to break a nylon rope. Later at home, I tied the rope up in the ash tree behind our farmhouse, stuck my foot in a loop at the end of the rope, and jumped up and down. The rope refused to break. There was a spiritual answer and it took me a long while to understand. In essence the Sacred Tree was saying, "I own you now, and you're not getting away easy."

I was weak, but toward the end I got stronger, and when I had broken free Uncle Bill came up to me. As he handed me back my bloody flesh pins he said in a low voice, "You're a great man."

At the time, I believed that he probably said that to all the dancers. I thought I had done poorly, and he was just saying that to make me feel better.

Later, after the dance and our final Sweat Lodge ceremonies were over, I was back at our camp, drinking soup and eating watermelon. All around us, people were breaking camp, getting ready to return home. Some had only a few miles to go, while others had half a continent to cross, as we did. At the Giveaway, money, food, blankets, and star quilts had been donated to the dancers and singers. The money was "gas money" to help the long-distance travelers get home. Some of them would never have made it without that generosity.

I saw Uncle Bill and Oray headed toward our camp. We welcomed them, offering watermelon and coffee.

After a couple of mouthfuls, Uncle looked at me, saying, "Hard, wasn't it? But you done good!"

Seeing the skeptical look on my face, he spoke forcefully. "No! Don't look like that! This was your lesson, your in'erduction. It'll take you at least a year to understand what happened to you." He repeated, as though to himself, "At least a year!" It took me two years to understand that the Sacred Tree had possessed me and wouldn't let me go, no matter how lightly I was pierced.

Pointing to his bare chest, Uncle Bill said, "See them scars? Twenty-six Sun Dances! It took quite a while for me t'understand!" Pointing to the puckered scars on Oray's chest, he added, "Six Sun Dances, an' he's still learnin'!"

With a sweet smile, Oray said in his husky voice, "Takes a while. You'll get it." Laughing softly he added, "Or it'll get you!"

We all had a good laugh, then sat quietly for a while. Paula's eyes were glowing. During the dance, Uncle Bill had called for all the mothers in camp to come to the center for a blessing and a healing. Paula had had an experience that made a believer out of her: her asthma was taken from her.

She told of how, when she had stepped across the invisible line separating the sacred inner dance area from the outer world, she had received an electric shock or jolt. Then, as we dancers had come past her and the other mothers, touching them with our hands or eagle feathers, she said that some of us had shocked her as we touched her. It felt like a static electricity shock, as one gets in winter from a car.

Two years later, Uncle Bill would give her an "honor" name, Holy Walker. At that time he would tell her that he couldn't teach her anything, that she already knew a great deal. It took her a while to accept it. Paula has been the women's leader of the Eagle Voice Sun Dance and Women's Circle for many years now.

Uncle Bill and Oray rose to leave. We shook hands all around. I thanked them for their help and support.

"When you come back next year, I want you to come to my camp. It's 'bout six miles east of here, off the road to Saint Francis." I told Uncle Bill that I would be back during my spring break the following year.

"You got a good truck? Not much of a road into my place,

'specially in springtime when it's wet. It's a couple of miles off the hard top." I told him I would find it.

"See you then! *Mitakuye oyasin.*"

I repeated the phrase.

After Uncle Bill and Oray left, Paula, Cody, Lame Deer—a young Aleut Indian who had been camping with us—and I packed our tent and gear into the old station wagon, said our farewells, and hit the road. Lame Deer was headed for Seattle, his home. When we got to Mission, he asked that we drop him on Route 83, so he could hitchhike south to Interstate 80.

"Hey, man!" I said, "that's close to two hundred miles of two-lane blacktop through the sand hills of Nebraska. Not much traffic on 83!" I tried to convince him to go north with us to Interstate 90, but he was sure he'd have better luck on 80.

We had just enough money to get home, but I gave him twenty-five bucks for food money. I wrote down our address and phone number and made him promise to keep in touch. He had come to Washington, D.C., on the "Trail of Self Determination" and had lived with us until we left for the Sun Dance. Two days after our family arrived at the Sun Dance, Lame Deer showed up, having hitched out from D.C.

During the seventies and early eighties Indians tried many times to get help from the politicians in Washington. Native Americans tried over and over to get the government to reverse or better many policies destructive to the Native population. The Trail of Self Determination was one of these efforts. Another was the Longest Walk, in 1978, which started from California. The walkers carried a sacred Pipe all the way to Washington, intending to present it to President Carter. Carter did not see them. Uncle Bill had filled that Pipe in California.

Now we sat in the car, watching Lame Deer with his thumb stuck out, until he got his first ride. He tossed his little pack— his worldly possessions—into the back of the pickup that had stopped, and waved goodbye. That was the last we ever saw or heard from him. Wherever you are, Lame Deer, I hope you're healthy and happy.

I put the car in gear and headed for our home sixteen hundred miles away.

Ghost Ramble

"No such thing as ghosts! Now go to sleep." That's what our folks told my brother and me, over and over. Didn't matter that we'd seen them, or one of us had seen them, in the attic of the 160-year-old farmhouse, or in the orchard, or even in the outhouse.

Brother Ben saw them climbing into bed one night and we awakened Pop with our fearful screams. After he had left us alone to try to go back to sleep, Ben described them to me. They had red hands, he told me.

Uncle Bill taught me about ghosts, or spirits. They're like people, he said. They get lonely, hungry, or ticked off just like us. They're happiest when people are enjoying life, celebrating, or praying. They like it when there's plenty to eat. The thing to do is to keep them happy by remembering them and feeding them.

"When they see that you're not stingy with your food," is what he said, "that you remember them by offering bits of your food, then they want to stay around and help you! They won't bother you then."

The problem is that people don't believe in ghosts, and they actually are stingy and scared. That really ticks off the spirits!

CHAPTER THREE

Uncle Bill's Camp:
The Valley of the Ghosts

During spring break the following year, 1977, I took off alone in my old '65 Chevy truck and drove to the reservation. The weather was fine till I crossed the Missouri River on I-90, when I began to see the remains of a big snowstorm piled up on both sides of the road.

The rolling, treeless plains slowly whitened as I wheeled westward, going as fast as the old truck would run. The sun was setting ahead of me, the sky hazed by high cirrus clouds.

Sun Dogs—rainbow-colored miniature suns—appeared on both sides of the sun and stayed there until sunset. I wondered what they meant. Turning south at Murdo, I highballed toward the reservation, hoping to get there before it was too dark.

Just north of Rosebud town, I was flying along between six-foot snowdrifts. The road had been plowed by the tribe. Suddenly, the road disappeared. My headlights picked up nothing but white.

"0-ohh, shee-ee-it!" I hollered, and jammed on the brakes.

There was just enough bare road for the brakes to slow the truck to about thirty miles per hour. Ahead of me was a ten-foot drift blocking the road. The tribal snowplow had cut only one six-foot lane through it. I whacked into the hole, the scraping of the truck on both sides slowing me just enough so that I stopped bumper-to-bumper head-on with another pickup. A whole family of Rosebuds—mom, dad, and three kids—glared at me through the windshield. The man was angrily gesturing for me to get out of the way.

The truck and I were stuck, like a cork in a bottle, wedged into the huge snowdrift. I couldn't even stick my head out the window; a wall of snow was pressing against the glass. The man turned to look out his back window, and I saw a couple of heads appear over the roof of his truck. The snowplow crew had jumped up onto the bed of his Ford and now looked at me with astonishment.

The crew hooked a cable to the other pickup and pulled it backward out of the cut. Then they winched me through the snowbank. I jumped out of my truck to apologize to the family for holding them up. By then, everybody was treating the incident as a huge joke. We all shook hands, laughing. The plow made another pass through the snowbank, opening up the road to traffic. The man and his family waved goodbye and continued their journey north. I said my thanks to the road crew and started south, passing through the town of Rosebud.

When I got to Grandpa Crow Dog's, where the Sun Dance had been the year before, the snow was too deep to drive into his place. I left the truck on the edge of the road and, in the luminous darkness of the snowy night, walked toward the light shining from the humble log shack. Grandpa was delighted to see me. Grandma put a big tin bowl of soup, a cup of coffee, and some saltines on the table and watched me eat.

Grandma Mary and Grandpa Henry lived in a one-room log

house about fifteen feet square. That evening there were three other people staying with them, sleeping on the floor.

"*Kola* [friend]," Grandpa said to me. "Too many folks here. Where can you sleep?"

In the back of my truck, I told him. The pickup had a cap on it and I had it fixed up for camping, with a sleeping bag and blankets. I told him about the Sun Dogs I had seen, asking what they meant.

"Gonna get cold tonight, Friend," he said. Grandpa Crow Dog never called me Grandson or Nephew, just "Friend." Out of respect I always called him "Grandpa."

After we talked a while, I said good night and went out to the truck. It was already way below freezing. The stars were twinkling in a brilliant black sky, and the smoke from the cabin's stovepipe rose straight up in the still, frigid air.

Inside my little camper I lit my lantern, put on all my clothes, and crawled into my sleeping bag, throwing an old quilt over the top. I turned off the lantern and, feeling warm and comfortable, went off to sleep.

I awoke at the first light of dawn, amazed to find the entire inside of the truck coated with a half-inch of delicate crystalline rime. The temperature inside the truck was zero. Outside it was twenty below. The moisture of my breath had condensed into hoarfrost. Even the top of the quilt was iced over. I ducked back into the warm sleeping bag for a few minutes. No use. My body demanded relief.

I unzipped the bag, stuck my feet into icy boots, and opened the tailgate, jumping out into the crunchy snow. Running to the outhouse, I answered nature's call in record time.

When I walked into the house with an armload of wood, everyone was still in the sack. The fire was nothing but hot ashes, and the temperature in the little cabin must have been close to freezing. I built up a big roaring fire.

As the sheet-metal stove began to glow, Frankie Shooter,

lying on the floor nearest the stove, rolled over and said, *"Pilamiya!* [Thanks!] G'morning!"

I asked him if he had run out of wood. He said that he'd been stoking the fire till three in the morning but had been "too chicken" to go outside for another load after the last piece had burned.

I got some water from the water bucket, after breaking the ice, and put on a pot of coffee. Grandpa stuck his head out of the pile of blankets he and Grandma were under and waved his arm in the direction of one corner of the room.

"Leciya." ["Over there."]

In the corner was a box of commodities. I got out bacon, flour, lard, sugar—all the makings of a breakfast. I put the bacon in a big spider—a cast iron skillet—and put it on the stove next to the coffee. In a few minutes, the smell of coffee and bacon filled the room, and people began to stir.

After breakfast, Frankie and I went outside and, using mauls and wedges, split up a good supply of firewood, which we brought inside and stacked near the stove. The day was warming rapidly, the snow melting off the roof and forming long, elegant icicles on the eaves.

The tribal snowplow arrived and cleaned up the road and the parking area around the house. By ten o'clock, Frankie and I were sweating, peeled down to our T-shirts. Around the entrance to the house, the trampled snow was turning to muddy slush. We brought a couple of buckets of fresh water from the river into the house, and sat down at the table for a coffee break. Grandpa joined us.

"Gonna cer'mony tonight. Lotta folks," he said. Referring to the woman for whom the ceremony was to be held, he continued, "she's bringin' the food an' offerings after noontime. So, you help out!"

Grandpa wanted us to cut more wood and help clean out the house, stacking the furniture outside and in the toolshed.

By four, we had removed all the furniture except for Grandpa and Grandma's big double bed and the woodstove. We had put blankets and pillows on the floor around the perimeter of the room for folks to sit on.

Mrs. Smith, the woman who was "putting on" the ceremony, brought a big pot of *wohanpi,* or soup, *wojapi,* or fruit pudding, a cardboard carton full of fry bread, along with big pots of *ceyaka*—mint tea—and coffee. There were also saltines and white bread and several pies. We stacked the food in the kitchen lean-to and in the corner of the room, next to the woodpile.

Toward sunset, people began arriving in old pickups and cars. I saw Uncle Bill and Aunt Hazel pull into the yard in his old blue Ford. I went out to greet them. Uncle asked me when I was coming over to his place. I said I would be there tomorrow.

By dark, twenty-five or thirty men, women, and children were standing around, inside and outdoors; the men together, smoking and drinking coffee, the women helping Grandma get ready for tonight's ceremony. Frankie and I, with some of the men, were busy tacking blankets over the windows, making sure the room would be pitch dark.

Nighttime ceremonies, done in a totally darkened room at night, are called *Lowanpi,* meaning, "They sing." But tonight's healing ceremony was to be a *Yuwipi,* meaning, "They tie him up." When someone is really sick they *Yuwipi* the medicine man, binding him so he is completely at the mercy of the spirits. If they don't respond to his entreaties for the sick person, come and untie him and heal the sick one, the medicine man might even die, suffocate.

Remember, the word *religion* has its roots in *religare,* "to tie up." The old Christian hymn says, "Blest be the tie that binds," but most Christians never truly get bound up in their religion. Jews have something similar, called *tefillin,* with which they symbolically bind themselves.

For the *Yuwipi,* an Altar is set up in the center of the room, the people sitting around it on the floor against the walls. The medicine man's assistants wrap him in a buffalo robe or star quilt. Before they do this, they tie his hands behind him with a rawhide bowstring. Then once he's wrapped, a rawhide noose is tightened around his neck. All told, he is tied up with seven knots from neck to ankles. Photographs of a Medicine Man tied up in this way can be seen in Richard Erdoes's book *Lame Deer, Seeker of Visions.*

The medicine man is like a mummy then, and he is laid down inside the Altar. Cloth offerings and 405 prayer ties—tiny bundles of tobacco offerings—surround him, marking the perimeter of the Altar.

Each medicine man receives his Altar from the spirits, representatives of the Great Spirit, usually during a prayer vigil on a hilltop. The Altar is received as a set of instructions on what he is to do and what materials to use. A man who seeks this Altar vision may have to stand on the hilltop many times, each time for four days and nights without food or water, before the spirits speak to him. That vision seeking is called *Hanblecia,* meaning, "Crying for a dream." Leonard, Grandma and Grandpa Crow Dog's son, who was to be tied for tonight's ceremony, had received his Altar up on Grass Mountain years ago as a young boy.

People began to settle themselves on the cushions around the perimeter of the room. Friendly small talk became a murmur then died out as Leonard and his helpers started setting up the Altar. Five long sticks were stuck into coffee cans filled with dirt, one for each of the directions, and one for the center. The upper half of the center stick was painted red, the lower half, black, with a thin white stripe separating the two colors. This stick and its supporting can of earth was positioned between the West and North sticks. The five sticks and earth-filled cans demarcated a square about six feet by five feet in the center of the room. This was the sacred precinct, or Altar.

Long cloth offerings in the four sacred colors—black, red, yellow, and white—were attached to the tops of the sticks. Mrs. Smith handed Leonard the string of 405 tobacco ties rolled into a ball. In the old days, the most precious possessions were tobacco and cloth, since these things were hard to come by. In any offering, if you are not giving flesh, you give the best you have, little bundles of tobacco wrapped in small squares of cloth the colors of the four directions. In older days, before cloth was available, the tobacco ties were wrapped in buckskin and called "buckskin tokens." They are prayers for enlightenment, health, endurance, strength, and growth. Whether for a *Yuwipi* or Vision Quest Altar on a hilltop, they are wrapped around the Altar as offerings and for protection.

When the Altar was completed, the sacred Pipe was filled, and Leonard handed it reverently to the Pipe holder, his mother, seated west of the Altar, in front of the red and black stick. Leonard's helpers tied him up. Silently, they lowered his mummylike body onto the Sage *(Artemisia sp.)* strewn in the center of the Altar. The singers tapped their drums, eager to begin. The light was doused.

Silence filled the velvet blackness of the little house. The drums roared to life as the singers began the Spirit Calling song. "Friends, I am calling you! From the West, the North, the East, the South. From Above and from the Earth, I am calling you! We need your help! I am calling you."

In the awesome darkness, we waited for the spirits to appear as the song was repeated, over and over again.

Something was stomping on the roof, scratching the tin stovepipe. A little light flickered near the ceiling, then dozens of lights were filling the sacred darkness all over the room. The spirits had arrived to untie Leonard and to help Mrs. Smith.

Most decent people at some time will pray for understanding, for enlightenment, for the light. The spirits come in the form of light, and not only for Indian people.

A big bird was flying around the room, brushing us with his wings. The spirits descended from the roof and stomp-danced around the Altar, shaking the little log shack. They clustered around Leonard. Leonard, his voice muffled from inside the quilt, spoke to the spirits. We saw the little spirit lights go to Mrs. Smith. We could hear tiny squeaky voices speaking to Mrs. Smith (they sounded something like Alvin the chipmunk).

After many songs, the Quitting song was sung and someone lit the lamp. Leonard was sitting in the Altar, the star quilt neatly folded, the rawhide rope, bowstring, and all the tobacco offerings rolled up and piled on top of it.

Everyone was blinking in the now bright light of the kerosene lamp. We all looked around the room, smiling. The sacred Pipe was lit and passed around, all partaking of the smoke. A bowl of water—the water of life and health—was passed, and all drank from it.

The helpers began passing out the food: *wohanpi* (soup), *wojapi* (fruit pudding), *ceyaka* (mint tea), fry bread, and more. Any leftovers were loaded into boxes and buckets called *watec'a* to be taken home by the participants.

At the end, everyone stood and said, *"Mitakuye oyasin!"* then shook hands and departed. It was about two in the morning as we stood in the yard saying our goodbyes, the starlight illuminating our faces.

Before he left, Uncle Bill said, "I'll see you tomorrow. Watch that road into my place. It's tricky."

"I'll be there," was my answer.

Late the following morning, I told Grandpa that I was going to pay Uncle Bill a visit.

"When you come back, you're always welcome here, *kola*," he said. I thanked him for his kindness to me.

I found the landmark Uncle Bill had told me about and turned off the road onto a track crossing the prairie. The snow was deep in spite of the thaw, and the going was difficult. The big-lugged traction tires on my old truck helped a lot. In a mile, I came to a steep downhill pitch and decided to walk it from there, not knowing whether I could make it back up the hill if I drove.

At the bottom of the hill, the lane entered a stand of scrub oaks and pines. I slogged along. On the side of the lane I came to an inverted car hood that had been rigged up as a sledge. A hundred-pound container of propane gas was on it. The steel cylinder and gas probably weighed two hundred pounds combined. I realized that this was the only way his helpers could get cooking gas into Uncle Bill's camp. Later, Oray told me that he had dragged that load as far as he could from the road, hoping I or someone else would come along to help him finish the job.

Walking through the heavy snow, I began to catch glimpses of a log house standing on the bank of a little stream. In front of the house, a large Sweat Lodge, Altar, and fireplace stood about forty feet away. The door to the log house banged shut as Uncle Bill stepped outside, squinting up the lane at me. Breathing hard from the long walk, I came up to him.

"*Hau*! It's you! You made it. *Was'te!*"

He led me into the log house. I greeted Aunt Hazel, who brought a big coffeepot and pound cake over to the old table. We all sat down.

"So. Did your scars heal up good from last summer? You ready t' dance again?"

I told him I was ready.

After coffee he got up, motioning me to follow, and walked outside.

In the warm sunlight, the snow was melting, the little creek gurgling with the meltwater. Uncle Bill pointed out the Sweat Lodge, the log house, and the high bluff across the creek. Up on top, he said, was *Hanblecia makoce*—Vision Quest ground. Around the log house were a collection of old surplus wall tents and small geodesic dome houses made of plywood where his students and apprentices lived.

"This here is Eagle Feather Culture Center," he said, waving his arm around at everything. "I made this for the people, so's they could come an' learn traditional ways. Right now our Sun Dance—Sioux Nation Sun Dance—is held up at the fairgrounds, but it'll be held here soon's we get the arbor built." The fairgrounds is where the Rosebud Fair takes place annually. The arbor there is used for rodeos and powwows, not reserved for sacred or ceremonial events alone. Uncle was uncomfortable having to share sacred space with commercial doings. Eight or ten years before, the Pine Ridge Sun Dance had been a sort of tourist attraction when Uncle Bill danced there. There had been words between the spiritual leaders and the tribal council, who wanted to exploit the ceremony, mixing it with a powwow and rodeo. After the Wounded Knee takeover in 1973, the more traditionally minded moved over to Crow Dog's on the Rosebud, and continued the dance there without the hassle of popcorn and Cracker Jack vendors.*

I asked him why he had chosen this particular place, so far away from everything.

"We could call this place Osmaka, a kind of a valley of the spirits. I came here because I wanted to work with these spirits. Sinte Gleska, or Spotted Tail, died near here, and Omaha Boy and John Strike, too—good medicine men. I ask them for help."

He walked up to a tiny egg-shaped turquoise travel trailer. "C'mon in here. We can talk in my trailer." He opened the door and climbed in.

---

*In 1973 Leonard Crow Dog was the spiritual leader of a group of Indians who took over a trading post and church in the tiny settlement of Wounded Knee, South Dakota, to protest the killing and brutalization occuring on reservations all over, but particularly on the Pine Ridge reservation. The siege lasted seventy-three days, with the Indians, armed with a few squirrel and deer rifles, facing off against a large group of FBI agents and American military personnel armed with modern weapons and armored personnel carriers.

At one point two federal agents claiming to be U.S. Postal inspectors gained entrance by saying they had to inspect the tiny post office in the trading post. Leonard was taken into federal custody, where he remained until 1976. This, in brief and without details, is approximately what occurred.

Inside, there was room for a bed, a compact kitchen, and a breakfast nook made of benches and table. We sat facing each other across the little table. Again, he was staring at me with his piercing glance.

"What's on your mind, Nephew?" he asked.

Words spilled out of me about everything that had happened since I was a kid that was incomprehensible to me. I told him about the spirits that had come to me at night, scaring me silly, on the hilltop back home. I begged him to help me understand these things—the white swallow, the black horse, the spirits who talked to my son, Cody, and me but whom only Cody could understand. I finished by telling him of the Spotted Man spirit who had stood in front of me on the hilltop in broad daylight, and how the eagle had brushed my face, twice, with his wings.

Uncle Bill's eyes dropped, and he studied in silence his big hands resting on the table. After a while, he resumed his wordless staring at me. I couldn't meet his eyes because tears were coming to mine. Being able to talk to him about these things at long last was a relief, and it stirred up emotion.

Breaking his long silence, he said, "I want you to dance with me this summer up at the fairgrounds. Oray'll be there to help you."

Then, "We're gonna have a Sweat tonight. I'll find out more in there. I'm gonna tell you everything I know. Do you want that?"

I would welcome it, I said. I asked him again for an interpretation of my dreams and visions.

"God gave you a brain, you figure it out!" That was all he said.

Later, I came to understand that this was his way of making his students work for their enlightenment. He used to say that if it was handed to me on a platter it would be meaningless.

As Uncle Bill and I left the trailer, Oray walked up with a

big welcoming smile. He and his wife had lived through the whole winter in a wall tent alongside the ceremony log house. How they survived in below-zero weather was beyond me. Uncle Bill told us to clean out the Sweat Lodge, to cut wood for the ceremony, and to make ourselves useful around the place.

As we worked, I asked Oray if he knew about the spirits Uncle had told me about, the medicine men who had caused him to settle here.

With a grin, he said, "You bet! They come around and scare me half to death, 'specially old John!"

He told of how last summer everyone had gone to a pow-wow, and he had stayed to guard the camp. That night, there was a full moon and he had gone to bed in the log house. Suddenly the door swung open. In the bright moonlight shining on the floor, he saw the shadow of a man. But there was no one standing in the doorway to cast the shadow. He said it was Johnny Strike's ghost but couldn't tell me how he knew. In abject fear, he pulled the covers over his head. When he looked again, the shadow was gone.

Toward evening, we lit the Sweat Lodge fire to heat up twenty-four rocks for the ceremony. At sunset in the freezing air, we stripped and entered the little Lodge. During the ceremony, Bill Eagle Feather prayed for me and everyone.

After we had finished and dressed and were having a smoke, he said, "Spirits say it's OK. We'll work together after the Sun Dance this summer."

A sacred process had begun that would last until Uncle Bill died on September 15, 1980. Through the influence of his spirit, it still endures.

Identity Amble

Many things go into making you who you are. A change of clothes, a change of hats, or a change of names may make a big difference in your life. Jamake Highwater talks about it in The Primal Mind. *In chapter 8, "Identity," Highwater speaks of the tribal custom of name giving. He begins the chapter with a quote from N. Scott Momaday, the Pulitzer-prize-winning Kiowa writer: "We are what we imagine. Our very existence consists in our imagination of ourselves . . . the greatest tragedy that can befall us is to go unimagined."*

I know of a guy, Clark Jones, who changed his whole life with a name change. He went to the courthouse and officially changed his last name to Kent. And he became, in a manner of speaking, Superman!

Popeye's statement suits me: "I yam what I yam an' that's all that I yam!"

CHAPTER FOUR

"You Ain't No Sioux!"

One day my artist friend Richard Klix said, "What the hell are you doing Sun Dancing? You ain't no Sioux! You're Danish!"

I told him I might not be Sioux, but I was as much Indian as Danish, which is to say, one quarter: an English grandma, a Danish grandpa, a grandma from the North Carolina mountains who died in 1924, the year I was born, and a grandpa we called Skipper from New York state, along the Hudson River. The North Carolina grandma was Cherokee, according to a vice-chief of one of the Cherokee clans who was an expert on genealogy. Maybe so.

Grandpa Skipper was a great old warrior and expert rifleman, and a long-distance runner with a gold medal and a gold watch to prove it. His farm was in Warren County, New Jersey, two miles north of Blairstown on the Stillwater road.

When I was five he said to me, "Boy! Time you learned to shoot."

He had an old High Wall Winchester match .22. It was bigger than I was. I couldn't lift it, so he put up a crotch to hold the rifle and taught me all about sight picture, breath control, and trigger squeeze. He must have had me put a thousand rounds from that old .22 into his maple log backstop. I got good at it.

On my eighth birthday, in 1932, my dad gave me a single-shot .22 Stevens rifle, and from then on I did my best to bring home squirrels, pheasant, quail, groundhogs, and other meat for the dinner table. This came in handy during World War II meat rationing.

On my eighteenth birthday, my dad presented me with a Winchester Model 92 in caliber 32-20, a takedown model that I still have. I later wanted to give it to my son on his eighteenth birthday, but he was still too wild to handle it. Sort of like his old man.

My brother, Ben, and I were both wild-hair-up-the-ass kind of guys. We had a succession of of four-cylinder Model A Fords that we tore around the countryside in, even before we got our licenses. Funny thing is, Paula, my wife, says it was my mom who was secretly very pleased with our wildness, and who encouraged it.

My dad used to take the license plates off the old Model A and strictly forbid us to go out on the road. We could drive it all over the farm, nowhere else. But there was an old set of 1940 plates hanging in the barn, which early on reflected my artistic talent by becoming '41 plates. And off we went into the night, the orange paint still wet on the plates, bugs sticking to it and getting whipped off by the wind. We even had some bartenders convinced we were of legal age. I was only five feet tall, 100 pounds, and baby faced, yet for some perverse reason I could drink my six-foot, two-hundred–pound kid brother and most of our friends under the table.

Drunk or sober, when I got out into the country alone, under the sun or under the moon, I had this overpowering feeling. It was of something infinitely greater than me, a spirit that was watching me, keeping me out of serious trouble. It took me many years to come to terms with and understand these feelings and visions. They came early, starting when I was seven.

After my dad gave me the single-shot .22, I would wander the fields and woods of my grandparents' farm. In summer, I would wear nothing to hunt, or just a pair of BVDs. Oftentimes I wouldn't kill the game but would simply sit very still, watching how the birds and animals behaved. I learned to call predators, foxes and hawks, by lip-squeaking, making the sound of a young rabbit in trouble. I found out that snakes are predators, too, when blacksnakes and a rattler came to my call.

During these times, the hot sun beating down on me, I got the feeling that we humans should be praying to the Sun, and not to some remote Christian God. These feelings are ultimately what led me to commit to Sun Dance.

After Pearl Harbor, I went down to enlist in the Army Air Corps. I was in love with flying. By age fourteen I had flown—or been allowed to control—my first plane, a beautiful Gull-wing Stinson Reliant. Later on, I did work for a couple of commuter airlines and in 1950 had some serious adventures flying as crew transporting Jewish refugees from Tehran to Israel.

"Too light," the sergeant said, looking over my medical data. "Go home and eat a lot of bananas." No matter how many pounds of bananas I ate, I couldn't make the minimum weight. Me, the crack shot and ace pilot, not allowed to use my valuable skills in wartime. I told the sergeant I was dying to be shipped overseas to kill me some Jerrys but it was no use, I spent the war toting an M1928 Thompson submachine gun in the 102nd Cavalry, an elite National Guard outfit that was the equivalent of the British Home Guard. We, the 102nd, were federalized, and all the runts (like me) and old men were left behind to guard the home front, which is what we did. Nazi saboteurs were rife in the minds of many, though few ever materialized.

While we read about the gallant men of the 102nd landing in Africa, Sicily, and Italy, then being split into two regiments for one to liberate Rome on June 5, 1944, and the other to storm Normandy the following day, we 102nd Cavalry stay-at-homes patrolled bridges, went through maneuvers (man, that Thompson was heavy!), got gassed by mustard, chlorine, phosgene, and tear gas (so we'd be able to identify the stuff in a real emergency), and took foolish orders from dumb lieutenants.

The dumb lieutenant stories were a great help fifty years later when I tried to help Vietnam vets suffering from post-traumatic stress disorder (PTSD). Sometimes it was the only thing to get them talking and laughing.

Around 1992 I got a phone call from Dr. So-and-So of the Richmond V.A. hospital. "We have an Indian vet who is suffering from PTSD. Do you do Sweat Lodge ceremonies?"

I told this doctor-psychologist that I didn't talk about those things to strangers and where the hell did she get my name? She told me that they'd called all over the East Coast to find someone and had finally given up and asked the Minneapolis V.A. Someone there had given her my name. I wanted to know who, but she had forgotten the name. Two years later I found out it was Harlan, one of my Sun Dance brothers.

Eventually, I gave this vet directions to find us, and Bobby showed up. He's been coming ever since and has been a great help to me and this place. The teachings I received from Uncle Bill that I pass on here at Eagle Voice Center have helped him and others.

How did I get from 1944 to this point? By getting ahead of myself. In my mind there's no time: 1944 and 2002 events are equally sharp and clear.

In between were my university education and years as a professional artist. Eventually my paintings and films wound up in many museums, including the Whitney Museum in New York City and the National Museum of American Art in

Washington, D.C. But my real education and achievement began at age fifty when Uncle Bill Eagle Feather, Grandpa Henry Crow Dog, and other kind elders started teaching me about *Lakol Wic'ohan*, the Indian way of life. I can tell you that a degree is a terrible impediment when an old man in a worn-out shirt and beat-up pants tells you that owls talk and lightning is your relative—even if you know he's a well-respected medicine man.

It took me quite a while, and some shocking experiences, before I realized that what I took to be Native myth or superstition had its basis in fact. When Grandpa Crow Dog was teaching me the Sweat Lodge ceremony, he started explaining the Powers of the World. He and I were alone in his Lodge. He spoke of the forces of lightning, the *Wakinyan* (literally "flyers," the thunderbolts and thunder gods) and the *Wakangli* (the particle of lightning power we have in our bodies), which come from *Wiyohpeyata*—the power of the West.

"They are powerful," he said, "scary. Their touch kills, but they're the ones that bring life to this Earth. We have to have a little of that *Wakangli* in us—not too much!—and when it leaves us we go back into the earth."

My attitude was, "What an interesting myth. We have to have lightning in our bodies and when it leaves we die."

A couple of months later I read in the science section of *Time* magazine that medical science now had a new definition of death: the absence of electrical energy in the body. I got goose pimples. "Holy Moses," I thought. "Those old Indians knew that before the scientists!"

That's when I really started paying attention.

My very identity as a teacher and practitioner of the Indian tradition stems directly from the ability I developed to pay attention to these great old teachers and their ideas.

Dog Romp

Things that are considered sacred by Sioux people, and other tribes, are just things—objects—to most folks; such things as plants, trees, earth, buffalo, buffalo dung, and dogs.

The dog story in this chapter isn't very sacred, but the dog is revered by Lakota people, particularly when used in connection with the Yuwipi, when it is ceremonially killed and made into wohanpi (soup). The spiritual relationship with dogs and dog soup is very old and may have to do with ancient times of starvation, when eating dogs was all there was between the people and death.

The medicine man paints the dog ceremonially, with sacred Wase, or paint. The young men strangle the puppy quickly; it must not feel any pain, nor must any blood be shed. The old women prepare, cut up, and cook the dog, and place the kettle in the ceremony house near the Altar. After the Yuwipi the soup is served, each participant eating of the dog.

CHAPTER FIVE

How the Dogs Chose Their Chief—or Didn't!

In June 1977, I was back in Uncle Bill's camp preparing for the Sioux Nation Sun Dance, the last time it was held at the Rosebud Fairgrounds.

Organizing any Sun Dance involves real problems in logistics. Sometimes one family will donate all the food for one day for all the spectators. There is usually one big meal put out each day for anyone there (except the dancers), and this could mean up to five or six hundred people. Someone will donate a beef, or a buffalo; someone will donate money. Someone might bring all the cloth offerings for the Sacred Tree, which usually consists of four, six, or seven eighteen-foot pieces of the sacred colors—black, red, yellow, and white; some spiritual leaders add blue, green, and violet. Cooperation and support are needed from many people.

This year, we had it pretty well together. The arbor at the fairgrounds is used for many things, especially rodeos and powwows, and the ground is pretty rough for dancing barefoot.

Thomas Mails, the author and artist, had donated sod so we could dance on grass. Of course, out there in that arid land they had to water the sod, and the tribe pumped water from the "lagoon" to do it (*lagoon* being the polite term for their waste-water pool, essentially a giant septic tank).

One evening during the four days of purification before the dance, we were sitting in the Sweat as the fire keeper brought us the rocks. The women sat in the back, the men on the west side toward the front. I know of three Sweat Lodge traditions: one says that only men sweat; another permits the women to have their own separate Lodge; the third, the one that Eagle Feather and Crow Dog practiced, allows men and women to pray (or sweat) together. Uncle Bill's vision told him to make mixed ceremonies, though during the eight days of the Sun Dance, we usually did sweat separately. This time, however, men and women were all in the Sweat Lodge together.

Uncle Bill called for the door to be closed. In the pitch darkness he began to pray. Suddenly, from the back of the Sweat, Aunt Hazel screamed and hollered, *"Mitakuye oyasin, Mitakuye oyasin!"* When the door was opened she threw out a slimy lizard that had crawled between her legs. The pumper truck had sucked up a few lizards with the water they'd gotten from the lagoon. Later, when the door was closed and the ceremony underway, I felt one crawling behind my butt. Quietly, I grabbed it and stuck it outside under the Lodge covers. I hated to think where they had been.

Leonard Crow Dog was going to be leader. The only thing that was rough was the weather. Sun Dancing, even on soft grass, is really hard in 110-degree weather.

There were not too many dancers. There was Oray, Chunzila, and Bad River Boy, a great favorite of Uncle Bill's, who would be tragically murdered the following year. The Hunger boys danced, and so did Reggy Left-Hand Bull. There were some I didn't know. Some had danced the year before in the same place. Their faces are to be seen in *Sundancing at Rosebud and Pine Ridge,* by Tom Mails. The support and camaraderie each of us gave and got still live in my mind.

My description of the Sun Dance is only partial. Mails's *Sundancing,* which Uncle Bill helped write and which features Uncle Bill, is much fuller.

My willpower and concentration were strong. I had learned a lot in a year. Even though I was pierced deeply, I broke free the first time. The rope and the pins flew all the way across the arbor. The breaking of the flesh sounded like whips cracking. I was relieved!

The older Hunger boy, who was about seventeen, got us a little squeamish during one of the rest periods. He had been pierced that round, and flies were feasting on his wounds and blood. Bad River Boy reached over to brush them off. Hunger knocked his hand away, saying, "You leave them alone! Them's my pets!" It was disgusting. We ganged up on him, trying to brush off the flies, but he fought us off, hollering that we had to leave his pets alone. There must have been fifty crawling around on his chest. He still had a few sticking with him all through the next round. He was hoping they'd lay eggs so he could have baby pets—also known as maggots! That boy was tough.

After everyone was pierced and the dance was over, Leonard led us out of the arbor back to the dancers' area and the Sweat Lodge. Leaving that grass and having to walk in a dignified manner over the sun-baked cinders and gravel outside the arbor was pure torture. We begged Leonard to let us run. Leonard, who was wearing moccasins, insisted on an orderly retreat. We were hardly dignified as we hopped along, trying to hit the candy wrappers and assorted trash—anything but those burning cinders!—to protect our blistered feet.

The red-hot rocks and steam of our final Sweat Lodge were a blessed relief, even on a hundred-plus-degree day.

After the Sweat we changed into street clothes, greased up our burnt feet, and sat in the shade of the brush arbor west of the dance circle, our thirst relieved by huge chunks of watermelon. Aunt Hazel and the women gave us all plenty to eat. It may seem strange that after all that fasting, none of us was very hungry. Watermelon and soda pop were what we all desired. And salt.

At sundown, we moved camp back to Eagle Feather Culture Center, and Uncle Bill resumed teaching us through his words and actions.

A couple of nights later, we had a *Yuwipi* ceremony in the log house. Uncle Bill made me sit next to Uncle Moses Big Crow. He wanted me to learn the songs, and Big Crow was a great singer.

When the ceremony was over and the lights came on, the young men in the group began to serve the food, *wohanpi*, the ceremonial soup made of dog meat. The guy who had the kettle didn't like me too much, and when he came to me he gave me the ass end of the dog. I must have had a funny expression on my face because Uncle spoke up in a loud voice, saying, "Henry! I want you to eat every bit of that! Geez! Here you guys from the East can eat all that disgustin' stuff from the ocean like oysters and lobsters, an' then you turn up your nose at a nice clean puppy dog. Well, it's beyond me." A big laugh ensued, at my expense. I dug in and ate it as best I could.

A few years after Uncle Bill's death I got even—sort of.

In 1984 I brought Harold, a Cherokee friend and retired army officer, to the reservation. We were involved in a *Yuwipi* for Uncle Moses. When the dog kettle came around, Harold, seated at my right, was served first. He got a foreleg; the paw, complete with claws, was hanging over the edge of his bowl. He stared at it, eyes wide, then at me. I said in a loud voice, "Harold, I want you to eat every bit of that! Geez! How you guys from the East can eat all that disgusting stuff from the ocean, like oysters and lobsters, and then turn up your nose at a nice clean puppy is beyond me!" Once again, there was a big laugh, this time at Harold's expense!

Bill Eagle Feather. He was a great man. Even today, more than twenty years after he left us, the medicine men talk about him at the Sun Dance. I could say that his whole life was a teaching, not only of the spiritual and cultural values of the Indians, but of how to actually live a moral life following the *Lakol Wic'ohan,* the Indian way. His teaching often took the form of jokes, practical and otherwise. Uncle Bill was a great believer in the humble life. When he taught me and others, he was particularly interested in bringing us down off our mental high horses.

When Bill Eagle Feather chose me as his student, it was an act of faith on his part, since I was not of his family or *tiospaye*—community. I didn't know that it would require an act of faith on my part to learn to accept his teaching.

He asked me if I wanted to learn. I had little or no faith in myself or in the things he could teach but said yes anyhow. He told me he was going to teach me everything he knew. In my self-important ignorance, I was flattered. I didn't know why I was the chosen one. I thought maybe his guardian spirit had told him whom to pick, or maybe he saw something in me. I was afraid that he had seen more than was there, that maybe I didn't have the stuff to accept the wisdom he wanted to pass on to me.

One evening we were getting ready for the ancient Sweat Lodge or breath of life ceremony. There were about ten of us there, ready for purification and renewal. In the back of Uncle Bill's big Lodge, there were three or four elder women, including his wife, Aunt Hazel, and Grandma Evelyn, the Sun Dance Mother. The front part near the door, as usual, was occupied by the men. I was sitting across the door from Uncle Bill to serve as his helper. Jerry, another of his apprentices, was the fire keeper. He would bring in the red-hot rocks from the fireplace and open the door when needed.

Uncle Bill began the ceremony by lighting a braid of sweetgrass, or *Wac'anga,* and handing it to me. I incensed the people and the interior of the Lodge. Uncle then filled the sacred Pipe, incensing each pinch of tobacco as he placed it in the pipe, and offering a pinch to each of the six directions, with prayers to the Great Spirit and to the Powers of his Creation. When the Pipe was filled, he handed it to Aunt Hazel, who held it reverently. He indicated to Jerry that it was time to bring in the rocks.

In a loud voice, as though speaking to a deaf person, he said to me, "Henry, I want you to pay attention! Jerry really knows how to handle these rocks an' I want you to learn somethin' tonight!" Jerry started bringing in the rocks. He did it the same way I did it. I couldn't see any difference. Putting twelve to eighteen twenty-pound red-hot rocks in a confined space filled with people is a potentially dangerous job that requires skill and finesse. As a fire keeper, I was a rank amateur next to Jerry, but I didn't know it.

When the rocks were all in place, Jerry handed in the bucket of water and closed the door tight, so there was no light visible. We watched one another in the red glow of the rocks. The rocks hissed and spat as Uncle poured on the water, a wave of hot steam rising all around us. Uncle Bill began his first song.

When the ceremony was over, we sat quietly cooling off in the fresh air coming through the door. Jerry squatted outside the door while we smoked the Pipe. "Well, Henry! Did you learn anything?" Uncle's voice boomed in the little Lodge. I thought it over. At that point I had my own Sweat Lodge and had been running the ceremony for several years back home. I believed I already knew it all, so I answered him, "No."

Uncle Bill's lips tightened. "Daggone it, Henry! How can you be so dumb?" The old women in the back tittered. Silently, the men looked intently at the ground in front of them. I could feel the blood rushing to my ears and cheeks.

Uncle went on, "Daggone it, Henry! Aren't you a college professor back East?" I muttered that I was, the anger and embarrassment growing till I was clenching my jaws. "An' you been a teacher how long?"

"Long time," I whispered into my lap.

"Well, then, how come you're so daggone stupid when you come back to the reservation?" Uncle Bill expelled a long, windy, exasperated breath. I didn't know what to say. He kept fixing me with a piercing look. "Well?"

I looked at him. "I guess I'm just a slow learner, Uncle."

Auntie and Grandma tittered again. One of the men glanced sideways at me quickly, then focused intently on the ground again. Uncle Bill said, "Well, you better fix that quick!"

"Yes, sir," I said.

After we left the Lodge, I was so steamed, so humiliated, I couldn't eat. I sat on the old rump-sprung couch by the Sweat while everybody chowed down on Auntie's fry bread and *wojapi.* After a while Jerry walked over, sat down beside me, and put his arm around my shoulders. "Hey, Henry! Don't feel so bad. I was a slow learner, too! He done that to me—lots." I began to feel a little better.

Over and over Uncle singled me out in similar ways. Sometimes he wouldn't use my name, but called me "the Dingbat" instead. He would say to one of the boys, "You an' the Dingbat take the pickup an' go get some sage down by the crick." I was grateful that the nickname didn't stick, and that none of the others joined him in calling me that.

When we were alone he treated me with the greatest kindness and generosity, gently repeating himself over and over when he needed to pass on some difficult piece of information. "Now—you got that?" he would say. If I didn't, he would patiently go over it again.

He was a pretty humble man in spite of his power and influence, so maybe he hadn't had to be brought down off a high horse by his own teachers, Fools Crow, Lame Deer, Pete Catches, and the others. He had been a journeyman electrician in California for a long while. He told me that before he got the call to return to the blanket, as they say—meaning, to the Indian way of life—he had tried to live the life of a white man. He even had a hobby, he said, of building and flying remote-controlled gas-powered model airplanes. But the spirits were bothering him so much in his dreams and in waking hours that he gave it all up, returned to Rosebud, and began walking the long trail that led him to be a spiritual man.

Part of that journey involved standing on Tipi Wakan, or Holy Lodge Hill, fasting and thirsting days on end for seven years. He was made a chief back in the sixties by those medicine men teachers for his part in restoring the Sun Dance. He was one of the first to publicly pierce in defiance of the government's ban. This was an act that could have landed him in jail; Indians, until 1979, were the only ones forbidden by law to practice their religion in this great country founded on the idea of religious freedom.

Bill Schweigman went through a lot of adversity in his life. Some Rosebud folks never let him forget he was only three-quarters Sioux, because he had a German grandfather. Behind his back they called him "half-breed" and even worse. At Sun Dances I heard him frequently praised after his death, but very infrequently during his life. I know it hurt him, but it also sharpened his will, and his wit.

A couple of days after the Sun Dance of '77, we were sitting around listening to a white man who was visiting Eagle Feather Culture Center. The guy was writing a book or something, and he had an elevated opinion of his own spirituality. He was full of stories about his dreams and visions and spiritual powers.

Uncle Bill listened gravely to his line of lingo, appearing to take it all very seriously. After a while the other guys and I began to cast furtive glances at one another, silently asking ourselves, "Is Uncle really swallowing all this crap?" We should have known better.

Finally, the guy asked Uncle Bill if he would interpret all this for him. Uncle rubbed his chin with a serious, thoughtful look, then asked the guy which hand he usually wiped himself with when he went to the outhouse, as if he were seeking more information to base his interpretation on. The guy said that, well, he usually used his right hand, but sometimes his left. There was a dead silence, then Uncle said, "I don't think I can help you. I usually use toilet paper."

The guy was a good sport and joined in our laughter. He also eventually learned a few things before he went back East.

Sometimes the jokes weren't aimed at anybody in particular, but they fitted in with the line of teaching he was pursuing. Three or four of us who were Uncle Bill's students sat around one day listening to him talk about the animals and plants. He was explaining how each community, or *tiospaye,* of plants and animals has their own leaders or chiefs, just as humans do. He taught us how to recognize them by their chief marks, and how to honor them, respect them. We were not to take the leaders but the others, after we had made the proper offerings. What he said was strikingly similar to what old Turkey had taught me about plant medicine back home.

"Course, there's one group that has never been able to choose their chief, an' that's the dogs. An' you guys can see 'em every day, still lookin' for their chief."

We wanted to know more. My son, Cody, then seven, heard the story when I got back home. It made a big impression on him. He later made a drawing of the story.

We were all out by the Sweat, Uncle lounging on the old car seat, the rest of us squatting in the dirt around him. We were waiting for the fire to make the rocks hot so we could begin a ceremony.

Uncle Bill pulled out a crumpled pack of Salem Lights and lit up.

"Well, long time ago the dogs had a big council meeting. They wanted to choose their chief, and different ones were making suggestions as to how to do it. This one good-looking warrior dog, he said that the chief should be the handsomest one. They all stared at him. One said, 'Yeah, you would say that, bein' as how you're so good lookin!' So they vetoed that idea.

"Another one—a big, heavy powerful bull he was—he said that the strongest should be chief. Same thing happened. They all put him down as lookin' out for himself. Well, this dog council came up with idea after idea, but everyone saw that the one with the idea was promotin' himself. Started gettin' late, sun was settin'.

Drawing done by the author's son, Cody Niese, when he was seven years old, illustrating Bill Eagle Feather's story of how the dogs chose their chief.

"Finally this one little runty dog piped up, 'How's about we pick for chief the one with the nicest smellin' hind end?' Well, that idea went over the top! Ever'body agreed on it. The council leader turned to his neighbor and sniffed his hind end.

"'Whew! Agh! This one ain't chief!' Then they all started smellin' each other's asses. 'Wow! Yuck!! Awful! Not this one!'

"They kept it up till the moon rose but couldn't find their chief. And they're still at it, lookin' for their chief. That's why ever' time two dogs meet they do that. They're still askin' each other, 'Are you the chief?' But they haven't found him yet!"

At the Center I Ramble

Years ago, somebody published a list of the most important words in order of importance. At the bottom of the list was the least important word, I. I and me were insignificant, according to this expert.

The Indian way, particularly the Lakota, teaches the opposite. Black Elk, Lame Deer, Henry Crow Dog, and many other wise men said, "You are the center of the Earth. Anyplace can be the center of the Earth."

The old Vision Quest song says, "This is me, this is me, this is me, this is me, behold me!" The singer-visioner dares to command the spirits' attention. The song declares that the singer-visioner's strength, purity of intention, and will, are worthy of sacred attention.

In a Christian setting (and others) such a seeker would be laughed or scorned out of church as an egotist.

The difference between a stand-up guy who'll lay it all on the line for his people and a wimp has nothing to do with ego. Rather, it has to do with strength, intention, and will. That's what the old Vision Quest song says: Maka c'okata nawajin yelohe *[At the center of the Earth I stand].*

CHAPTER SIX

Hanblecia:
Crying for a Dream

In June 1978 Uncle Bill called from Rosebud.

"Time for you to *Hanblecia* the old-fashioned way, Nephew. I'm comin' out there to put you up on the hill for a Vision Quest. Can you send me a airplane ticket?"

I had talked to Uncle about the many times I had gone up on the hill behind my farm, and about the visions and spirits I had seen there. In the early seventies, when Cody was only two or three, he and I had slept up there. Cody had seen the spirits, too. Now Uncle Bill wanted to teach me the traditional Lakota way of *Hanblecia*—crying for a dream or vision.

After asking him what day he wanted to travel and when he wanted to return, I told him there would be a ticket waiting for him at the Pierre airport. He said that he would get a relative to drive him to Pierre.

A few days later, I was at the gate at Baltimore-Washington International, waiting to greet Uncle Bill as he walked off the plane. He was wearing an old jacket and wrinkled baggy pants.

He had a big spotted eagle feather in his hair. But his long gray braids were what made people stop and stare. He carried his *wopiye*, or medicine bag.

"Hau, Tunkska! Lila was'te!" ["Hello, Nephew! Good to see you!"]

His massive figure towered over me as we walked down to retrieve his bags.

As we drove home in my old pickup, he began to lay out the details of the coming *Hanblecia* ceremony. He said it would be good if I could arrange to have seven people help me—even better if they were of all ages, from youth to elders. I told him of Turkey, the old Piscataway medicine man who had been helping me and teaching me about plant medicine. There were also several young people who wanted to help.

"Good! Now, you're gonna need four hun'erd an' five tobacco ties, four cloth offerings, four cherry or cedar trees—watch out for that truck!"

I braked hard to avoid a six-wheel van that had pulled into my lane without signaling. Uncle gave the young driver an icy glare as we passed him.

Uncle growled. "He musta got his license in a Cracker Jack box!"

Then, switching to his normal tone, he picked up where he'd left off. "An' a blanket, some sage, an' a couple other things. You got your *Cannunpa* [the sacred Pipe]? I'll be fillin' it for you."

As we pulled into the drive back at the farm, Cody ran out of the house, shouting his greeting to Uncle Bill. They hugged each other. Cody was seven now, and he and Uncle got along beautifully. One day, Paula had found some *Playboy* magazines under Cody's bed, probably lent to him by an older friend. Uncle Bill ragged Cody playfully about his reading habits. Come Christmas time, Cody had me buy him a *Playboy* to send to Uncle Bill. In his childish scrawl, Cody wrote on the enclosed card, "Merry Christmas from one Playboy to another."

After coffee and cake, we walked out back to the Sweat Lodge. Eagle Feather said we would have to make a few changes to bring it up to snuff. In following Uncle's instructions we wound up rebuilding the whole thing, pulling the covers off and tearing out the old willows and replacing them with new saplings.

"*Ohan!* [Yes!]," he said, while surveying our handiwork. "Now you got a real Sweat Lodge!"

The next day, we went to southern Maryland. I wanted Uncle Bill to meet Turkey. Turkey was waiting for us, the door to his shack open wide.

"Come right in, set yourselfs down. Coffee's ready. Got some fatback and a leetle corn cake here, too. Good to meet you! Wild Goose's been tellin' me all about you!"

We sat down at the little kitchen table. Turkey set the food and coffee before us.

Peoples from different tribes seem to have an inborn suspicion of one another. The food, the customs, even the tobacco are different. The big-leaf Virginia and Maryland tobacco is not even considered tobacco by some tribes. I could see that Turkey's actions, food, and way of talking weren't sitting well with Uncle Bill. Later, he told me confidentially that he thought Turkey was a phony, and that I should stay away from him. Although I expected it, I was greatly amused when Turkey quietly told me the same thing about Uncle Bill. In the end the two of them would become good friends during my Vision Quest ceremony.

As Uncle and I left, Turkey agreed to help with my ceremony and said that his wife, Martha, would also help. We all shook hands.

The next day was spent getting everything ready for the *Hanblecia*. The word is overlaid with meaning but is generally translated as "crying for a dream or vision." The words for *cry* and *pray* are the same.

Usually, a person's first time up on a hill lasts for one day and night. By the fourth time, the quester spends four days and nights. Uncle was starting me out with two days and two nights.

Uncle Bill and I walked out into the countryside and chose four red cedar saplings, made tobacco offerings to them, cut them down, and brought them back to the Sweat Lodge. We tied the four cloth offerings to them. He commanded me to renew the earth Altar that stands between the fireplace and the Lodge, saying that it should be made of a simple mound of earth, looking freshly dug, like a molehill, with no adornments. I got down on my knees and began to clean the mound and renew it.

He inspected it when I was through. It had become a perfectly formed conical mound of fresh earth, like the ones the mole digs up, a humble Altar to our Mother Earth.

"*Was'te!* [Good!]," he said. "This is the molehill, the messenger of our Mother the Earth."

The mole represents Earth, as the eagle is the representative of Father Sky.

The Indian way of worshiping is the humble way. No gold-plated chalices or other expensive accoutrements. The church is a small Sweat Lodge dome. We come to that church naked, with only a towel for modesty. We sit on our Mother Earth after crawling in on our hands and knees. We call on the powers of *Wakantanka,* the Great Spirit, God Almighty, to join us there and hear our prayers.

Seven helpers were needed to send me on my way by "visioning the rocks," or gazing at the rocks for prophetic visions before they were put into the fire for the *Inipi* ceremony. Five young men, my wife, Paula, and Turkey's wife, Martha, would

Bill Eagle Feather in front of the Capitol Building, Washington, D.C., 1978. Photo by Henry Niese.

Author Henry Niese, his wife, Paula, and their son, Cody, after Henry danced at Crow Dog's Sun Dance on the Rosebud Reservation, South Dakota, 1976. Photo by Richard Lew.

Henry and Mary Crow Dog's House, Grass Mountain, South Dakota, 1976; site of the *Yuwipi* ceremony described in chapter 3. Photo by Henry Niese.

Grandpa Henry Crow Dog in his house, holding an eagle feather and sacred Pipe, 1976. Photo by Henry Niese.

Henry Niese sitting in his Sweat Lodge with Pipe praying for Leonard Crow Dog—winter, 1975, temperature at fifteen degrees below zero. Leonard was in a Federal penitentiary for leading the 1973 protest at Wouded Knee. He had requested Henry's prayers. Photo by Richard Lew.

Henry Crow Dog, Bill Eagle Feather, and Wallace Black Elk perform a ceremony in Digmann Hall, St. Francis, South Dakota, after Leonard Crow Dog's release from the federal penitentiary, 1976. The four bowls contain sacred food. Bill Eagle Feather's funeral wake was held here several years later. Photo by Henry Niese.

Henry Niese's first Sweat Lodge built at home in Glenelg, Maryland following Henry Crow Dog's directions—*heyoka* style—everything backwards from how it's traditionally done. Photo by Henry Niese.

Henry Niese, Bill Eagle Feather, Paula Niese, and Cody Niese in front of the Niese farm Sweat Lodge, 1978. Photo by Richard Lew.

Aunt Hazel, Uncle Bill Eagle Feather's wife, with sage crown at the 1975 Sioux Nation Sun Dance at Rosebud Fairgrounds, Rosebud Reservation, South Dakota. Photo by Greg Pietz.

Uncle Bill Eagle Feather having 200 pieces of flesh cut off his arms by Sun Dancers as offerings to the Great Spirit, 1975. From left to right: Yellow Hawk cutting, Evelyn Staub receiving flesh, Bill Eagle Feather, Black Feather cutting, Aunt Hazel receiving flesh, unknown participant. Photo by Greg Pietz.

Uncle Bill leads Aunt Hazel with a sage wristlet at the 1975 Sioux Nation Sun Dance at Rosebud Fairgrounds. Photo by Greg Pietz.

Oray Farrell after piercing at the 1975 Sioux Nation Sun Dance at Rosebud Fairgounds. Oray was Bill Eagle Feather's apprentice. He helped Henry Niese when Henry danced for the first time at the 1976 Sioux Nation Sun Dance (the last to be held at the Rosebud Fairgrounds) and at every dance after that. Photo by Greg Pietz

Lifting the Sacred Tree into place in the center of the dance arbor at the 1975 Sioux Nation Sun Dance. Here the tree is almost vertical with its cloth offerings flying. Photo by Greg Pietz.

Evelyn Staub, Sun Dance Mother of the Year, wiping blood from Rube Fire Thunder's chest after he has broken free from the Sacred Tree at the 1975 Sun Dance. Photo by Greg Pietz.

Eagle Feather Culture Center, Rosebud Reservation, Rosebud, South Dakota, with Sweat Lodge frame in foreground and log ceremony house behind. Dance arbor is just visible in upper left-hand corner. Henry Niese took this photograph in 1993, thirteen years after Bill Eagle Feather's death.

Wall tents at Eagle Feather Culture Center in 1978. Oray Farrell and his wife, Phyllis, spent the entire winter in a wall tent that year. Here, Aunt Hazel buttons up one of the tents. Photo by Henry Niese.

Bill Eagle Feather and Turkey Tayac trading stories at the Niese farm in Glenelg, Maryland before Henry Niese's Vision Quest, 1978. Photo by Henry Niese.

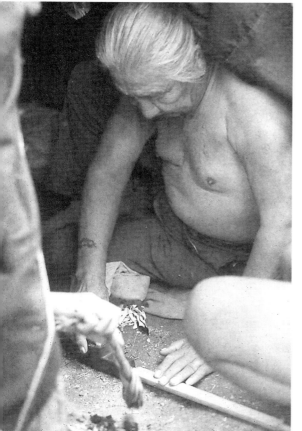

Bill Eagle Feather filling Pipe in the Sweat Lodge prior to Henry Niese's Vision Quest, Glenelg, Maryland, 1978. Photo by Henry Niese.

Bill Eagle Feather
taking forty pieces of
flesh from Henry Niese
in preparation for his
Vision Quest in 1978.
Photo by Kirk Talbott.

Richard Lew, Jim Boone,
and Paula Niese offering
flesh as a prayer for Henry
Niese's Vision Quest,
1978. Photo by Kirk
Talbott.

Proceeding to the hilltop where Henry Niese would complete his Vision Quest, Glenelg, Maryland, 1978. Henry has ceremony robe draped over his shoulders and Bill Eagle Feather carries a red cedar tree tied with the red cloth offering. Photo by Kirk Talbott.

Henry Niese surrounded by prayer ties before his 1978 Vision Quest. Photo by Kirk Talbott.

The entire 1979 Sioux Nation Sun Dance line at Eagle Feather Culture Center, Rosebud, South Dakota. Photo by Bill Eagle Feather, taken with Paula Niese's Brownie Instamatic camera after Eagle Feather confiscated all cameras for the duration of the Sun Dance. The image here is actually two photos spliced together. From left to right: Oray Farrell, Pete Spotted War Bonnet, Henry Niese, unidentified participant, Reggie Left Hand Bull, Manuel Left Hand Bull, Aunt Hazel, Phyllis Farrell, Nida Spotted War Bonnet, Paula Niese, Sandy Nanticoke Romie Encinas, and two unidentified girls

Lowanpi ceremony in the cellar of Henry Niese's Maryland farmhouse, 1978. Bill Eagle Feather, center, has set up his earth Altar, four sticks with colored flags, and the center stick. The square drum in the background is similar to Sitting Bull's. Photo by Brian Keenan.

Log ceremony house at Eagle Voice Center, Glenelg, Maryland; building completed in 1984. Photo by Henry Niese.

Interior of log ceremony house at Eagle Voice Center. Sun Dance skirts hanging on back wall. Cushions around perimeter for ceremony participants. Photo by Henry Niese.

Henry Niese presenting the sacred Pipe to Pipe Keeper during the 1987 Eagle Voice Sun Dance, Glenelg, Maryland. Photo by David Pankratz.

Altar mound with ceremonial equipment at Eagle Voice Center, Glenelg, Maryland. Left to right: Pipe bag, antler, eagle wing fan, stem and bowl of Pipe, sweetgrass braid, cedar bag, poker, another antler, tobacco bag, and another Pipe bag. Photo by Henry Niese.

Dance line at Eagle Voice Sun Dance, Glenelg, Maryland, 1988. The first two dancers left to right are Henry Niese and Cody Niese. Photo by David Pankratz.

Men blowing whistles on the 1990 Eagle Voice Sun Dance line, Glenelg, Maryland. The woman in wheelchair is asking for a healing. Photo by David Pankratz.

Council Circle and Fire, 35' in diameter, constructed by Henry Niese and Jim Bombino of 2' x 10' planks and tree stumps, 1995. Photo by Henry Niese.

Mystery Arbor, 18' by 9', constructed by Henry Niese of tree trunks and pine boughs, 1987. This arbor was constructed as an art installation—an evocation of the Sun Dance arbor—at the University of Maryland art gallery. Photo by Henry Niese.

assist. The men were Kirk, from Ohio; Brian, from upstate New York; Richard and Ben, sculptors from Maryland; and Jim, from the North Carolina mountains. The two medicine men, Turkey and Uncle Bill, would interpret the visions that the helpers would see in the seven chosen rocks.

Cody and other young children were there as we began. The Four Generations were present.

"Stand on the north side of the fireplace!" Uncle Bill commanded me.

He told the seven readers to stand on the south side. About twelve rocks were lined up in front of them on the south rim of the fireplace. Turkey and Uncle Bill stood in front of the fireplace.

Eagle Feather directed the helpers. "*Wana* [now], each of you choose your rock."

The helpers carefully looked over the rocks and each slowly picked one up.

"Now, look at your rock, an' tell what you see."

Visioning the rocks is a form of prophecy. If everything went right I would, at some time during my two days on the hilltop, experience something related to what the helpers saw in the rocks.

Eagle Feather called on Richard first. "Tell us what you see. Don't think, about it, just say the first thing that you see."

Richard saw a buffalo. Uncle looked at me to see if I got it. No interpretation needed. Paula was next: a deer chased by a wolf biting the deer's rear end. No interpretation. Ben saw a blind man trying to say something. Kirk saw a blind woman. Both Turkey and Uncle stared at me intently. My look told them I needed interpretation.

Uncle turned to Turkey. "Well, Cousin, what do you think?"

The use of the familial term let me know that Uncle and Turkey had formed a relationship. It made me very happy.

Turkey cleared his throat and said in his measured way,

"Well, Cousin, alls I know's that when the blind follow the blind, they's all gonna land in the ditch!"

Both their heads swiveled around. Both glared at me with their piercing eyes, as if to say, "You better get that straight!"

The image of Breughel's great painting *The Blind Following the Blind* flashed in my mind. I was sure that neither medicine man knew of the existence of this painting, which so graphically depicted Turkey's interpretation. Both Turkey and Breughel were warning of the disasters implied in that vision.

Martha was next. "I don't know why, but I see a beehive."

Uncle looked at me, saw that I needed help, and tersely said, "Bees take care of their own!"

As I came to understand that simple statement later on, it became the basis of part of my teaching. The whole world is failing to take care of its own, one of the reasons we're in such a mess.

Next was Jim, who quietly said, "Crying hawk." I didn't need an interpretation.

Finally it was Brian's turn. "I see nothing," is what he said.

The two gray heads once again turned and stared at me.

"God gave you a brain, you figure it out," was Uncle's response to my puzzled look.

It took me years to understand the power of nothingness.

Paula walked into the fire pit, placed four long pieces of wood oriented east-west in the center of the pit, then four more running north-south on top of them.

Eagle Feather got out his *Wase*—the sacred red paint—and painted a mark on each of the chosen rocks.

"Now, put your rocks on the fire."

Paula took each of the rocks handed to her by the helpers and placed them carefully on the wood in a cross formation, indicating the four directions. Armloads of dry wood were added to the pile, forming a large *tipi*-shaped pyre. After a prayer, the fire was lit, and it began to crackle and roar.

Eagle Feather took off his shoes and entered the Lodge. I handed him my Pipe. Paula lit *Wac'anga*—sweetgrass—and held it for him as he prayerfully filled the Pipe, incensing each pinch of tobacco, and offering it to the four directions, the Above, and Mother Earth. He chewed up a ball of sage and sealed the Pipe with the wad.

He crawled out of the Lodge, put the Pipe on the Altar mound, and asked me for the razor blades and needles. I handed them to him. I was going to make *ceh'pi waonye*—an offering of forty pieces of my own flesh to *Wakantanka*.

Eagle Feather picked up my Pipe, handed it to me, and instructed me to stand facing west in front of the Altar mound. I began praying. He began cutting flesh from my upper arm, offering the first piece to the six directions, imploring the Powers to behold my sacrifice. He took twenty pieces from my left arm, handing them carefully to Paula, who wrapped them in red cloth.

I could feel the blood running down my arm and dripping off my elbow. I could never stand the sight of my own blood—other people's doesn't bother me at all—and that drip-drip feeling was making me feel funny. I hung onto my filled Pipe, praying hard for mercy from the Above.

Uncle started on my right arm. When he finished, I was dizzy. Richard gently helped me into the Sweat. I sat in the *Catku*—the place of honor in the back. What happened next, I can only ascribe to the spiritual intensity and emotion I had been going through.

There is another world, and it is one with this one. It could be called the visionary world. In a lifetime, if one is lucky and does everything right, one might spend a few seconds there, and those few seconds will last a lifetime. It is a world of light and intense color. In those few seconds, the visioner will see and understand the great preciousness of the most common, ordinary things, things we spend a lifetime ignoring or taking for granted. The Indians say, *"Maka kin le wakan."* ["This

Earth is sacred."] Those seconds help us understand what that means. They also make the meaning of *joy*, *praise*, and *rejoice* clear in our lives.

I experienced those few incredible seconds sitting there in the *Catku*, waiting for the ceremony to begin. The grains of sand and earth before me in the center of the Sweat Lodge were transformed into the most precious things, more beautiful than gold and jewels. The light of the afternoon sun pouring through the low door of the Lodge was transformed into torrents of delicate, rich soft color, with pale green and light fuchsia-pink predominating.

Lao-tzu said, "The Tao that can be spoken is not the eternal Tao." There are no words to describe, and words only confuse. When it happens to you, you will know it. My words can only poorly suggest what happened there and during other visionary experiences I have had.

Outside the Sweat, unbeknownst to me, Paula and the others were all offering flesh that my Vision Quest be fruitful.

I sat in the back in another world, hanging onto my Pipe, as everyone crawled into the Lodge. The cedar, sage, and sweetgrass were handed in by the doorkeeper, along with the deer antlers used to position the red-hot rocks.

"Bring in those rocks!" Uncle Bill ordered.

They came in, one by one. I touched my Pipe to them, a way of asking the spirits for help. A bucket of water and a dipper were handed in. Then also one by one, the four trees with their cloth offerings were handed in, passed from hand to hand, and back out the door, the steam purifying them. The door was closed to leave us in darkness except for the glow of the rocks. Uncle poured water. A rushing sizzle of hot steam surrounded us as Uncle began his song. I shook to the vibration of his powerful voice. He sang the old Vision Quest song.

"Kola, le miye ca. Waun welo!" ["Friends, this is me. I'm coming!"]

The song is directed to the spirits, messengers of the Great Spirit, who are called Friends. They were supposed to come help me as I stood on the hilltop two days and two nights with no food or water, praying.

After the purification Sweat, I was solemnly paraded to the hilltop a quarter-mile behind my farm, the helpers carrying the trees, cloth offerings, and tobacco ties. I had my Pipe and a blanket, nothing else to sustain me for two days. I was feeling strong, brave, and a little heroic. My humbling came the next day.

The red cedars were planted in the ground, delineating a five-by-six-foot rectangle. The Altar for my Pipe—two small forked sticks supporting a crosspiece—was set up on the west side of the rectangle. *Pejihota*—prairie sage—was strewn to cover the whole area, and the tobacco ties were wound around the four trees, enclosing the rectangle of the whole Altar. I was, as they say, "tied inside" for the two days. The tobacco ties surrounding me looked a little like a barbed wire fence to protect me from the bad spirits and to attract the good ones.

Uncle Bill finished his instructions by telling me that, if I had to pee, to drape some of the sage over the ties and "hang it outside." He handed me a small pickle jar filled with water and a root.

"This is your medicine," he said, indicating the root. "Find out what it's to be used for."

He never said a word about the water. I believed at the time that it was another temptation for me to resist. Now I wonder if he thought I didn't have the strength to make it without any water and was just being kind to me.

It was Friday afternoon.

"See you Sunday. *Tunkasila nici unweyepo* [May the Grandfathers take care of you]."

I watched their figures diminish into the distance. Then,

pointing the stem of my Pipe to the West, I began to make my prayers.

"Grandfather West, Thunder Nation, this is me, I'm coming. Standing here I face you, asking for mercy and help."

I was wearing my Sun Dance skirt and traditional crown made of sage. It was the same skirt made for me a few years before by Diane Crow Dog, Leonard Crow Dog's sister, for my first Sun Dance. On one of the long pieces of sage sticking out of my crown, the one above and directly in front of my eyes, a honeybee landed. She sat there, four inches from my face, staring me in the eyes all during my prayers to the West. I remembered what Martha had seen in her rock, and Eagle Feather's words. I was surprised at how quickly things were happening. I said a prayer for Diane and her family. A light west wind was blowing in my face.

After a while, I turned and faced North. "Grandfather North, Buffalo Nation, this is me, I'm coming. I stand here and face you." I prayed for healing, renewal, and purification for all my relations. I was surprised by a puff of wind out of the north. It was as though the Power of the North were acknowledging my presence.

To the East, I prayed. "Morning Star Nation, Daybreak Nation, Elk and Deer Nation, this is me. I'm coming." I gave thanks for the light of day and prayed for the light of spiritual wisdom for myself, the world's leaders, and all my relations. Again, a breeze blew in my face. I felt my prayers were being heard.

Turning South I prayed, "*Tunkasila Itokagata* [Grandfather in the direction we always face], Animal Nations, have mercy on me, Great Spirit, and on all my relations. Give us the strength and joy to always keep to the good road so that we can face you to the end." Momentarily, the South wind blew in my face.

Returning to the West, I lifted my Pipe and prayed to the

sky, a simple prayer my friend Everett Brokenrope had taught me. "*Wakantanka Tunkasila onci malaipo.* [Grandfathers, pity me, help me, teach me.] I give thanks for your precious gifts."

Kneeling down, I put my mouth to the Earth. "Grandmother and Mother of us all, this is me, your grandson. Have mercy on me, help me, teach me to walk with respect on your precious face. You have given us everything, and everything we need comes from you. Thank you for the medicine, the food, and everything. Don't ever abandon us. We need you, I and all my relations."

There was much more that I said and prayed. Sometimes the prayers were voiced, other times they were expressed as thoughts. The beauty of the loneliness of the surrounding countryside overwhelmed me. Although I had lived here for the past ten years, I spent a lot of time meditating on the fields and trees. The round had taken about four hours. I stood up and, facing West, began again.

Over and over I repeated the round—West, North, East, South, Above, and Below—following Eagle Feather's directions. The words became meaningless. They didn't matter. What mattered was to entreat the Powers over and over to convince them of my sincerity. Each time I faced a direction, thoughts would come, and I would include other friends and relatives in my prayers. Facing West, I prayed for my departed relatives and friends—my grandparents, my father, my teachers, and all my relations. Facing North, I prayed for all the sick and imprisoned of the world. I prayed for my mother, my wife, and my two children, Robby, my daughter by my first wife, and Cody.

Facing East, I prayed for enlightenment for all the world's leaders, and for the peace that comes with understanding. Facing South, I prayed for health and growth for the world's children, and all my relations. *Mitakuye oyasin*—all my relations. That was the key, the reason I was there: to make relations with the Powers of the world, and to pray for my relatives.

I hadn't had any water since early morning. The setting sun was still so hot. My mouth was dry. I chewed on some sage, its bitterness relieving my thirst momentarily.

Round after prayer round I made. I knew I was supposed to keep standing, facing the directions, praying for help, in spite of how tired I was. The sun was near the horizon. My back and legs hurt.

As I faced South, without warning, a tiny hummingbird zipped up the hill and stopped, hanging motionless in the air in front of my face, staring at me. She chattered loudly. Then, too fast for my eyes to follow, she was gone. She had startled me. My heart was hammering. I began Sun Dancing, my feet stomping the ground. Strength surged through me, and a great feeling of joy came over me. A moment before, I had been seriously doubting that I had the will to continue. Now I felt I would be all right.

The sun set, and quiet evening darkness descended. I saw the first star. I was facing West, watching the afterglow, when a little bird came and began to sing a beautiful song from the chokecherry to the north. She was so close to me, yet I couldn't see her. This was what the old-timers would call an "encouraging song." The bird was helping me with her song.

I stood in the center, praying until full night came and the stars were very close. Then, groaning a little with weariness, I lay down under my blanket on the sage-covered ground and stared up at the stars.

It was hard to sleep on the rough ground; it was meant to be hard. I slept very little. Around midnight, I got up and began my rounds again, my blanket on my shoulders. Owls talked in the trees a hundred yards away. In the starlight, I looked at the jar of water and the root standing next to my Pipe rack. The clear water was tempting. I vowed not to drink a drop of it.

Picking up the root, I spoke to it, "Little relative, you are meant to help the people. I know a lot of your relatives, and what they are good for. I don't know you. Help me to understand how to use you for promotion of health and life."

The root lay silent in my hand, looking a little like a dancing figure. I put it back down by the Pipe Altar. Putting my Pipe on its rack, I squatted down, staring at the root. Nothing.

The night was awesome. Again and again, I would catch a glimpse out of the corner of my eye of a figure standing close by, watching me.

"Ho Tunkasila!" I would greet the spirits as Eagle Feather had taught me. Out of respect, one was not supposed to look at them directly. I tried it a few times, but they vanished. Sometimes I saw that the spirits were standing in the cedar trees. The experience made me understand why so many Indians have to work hard to overcome their fear of the nighttime *Hanblecia*. Standing alone on a hilltop in the dark was a scary thing to do.

"The filled Pipe is powerful, like a loaded gun," Uncle Bill had taught. "If you sense any of them spirits is bad, just point your Pipe at them and tell them to scat."

I had that bad feeling only once. My Pipe chased it away.

The singing of the birds before dawn woke me. I stood up. When I swung around to face the East, I saw the Morning Star—*Anpao Wic'ah'pi*—the Star of Understanding, hanging low in the sky with the faint rose of dawn under it.

"O Morning Star, first light of dawn, have mercy on me," I prayed. "Help me to understand why I am here and where I am going from here. Let your light of holy wisdom enter my mind and heart. Help me to be who I'm supposed to be, and do what I'm supposed to do, for all my relations."

I continued to make my rounds, the dawn light growing brighter. Just before the sun broke over the horizon, a flock of six Canadian geese silently flew over my head. They were so close I felt the wind from their wings. I was their namesake since Turkey had given me the honor name Go-yom-ac, or Wild Goose. Only the eagle was higher. I greeted them wordlessly, thanking them for their grace.

The day became hot, the sun boring down on me and the wild plants surrounding me. I wondered how they could take it day after day. Their endurance gave me courage. There was no shade. The little cedars at the corners of my space wilted.

Going for four days and nights without water in the Sun Dance was different. There's plenty of company in the Sun Dance, and all are suffering together. Misery loves company. Alone on the hilltop, I could draw only on my strength from within, and on the grace of the spirits.

I found the little pebble tucked into my skirt that I had sucked on during the Sun Dance. It helped some, and the leaf of sage helped. Still, my mouth slowly dried completely. I kept on praying, dancing, stamping on the Earth, asking Grandmother to send me strength.

I felt the power coming to me from my feet and legs! She was answering my prayer.

In midafternoon, facing West, I was praying for the spirits of my grandparents who had died many years before. The tears were rolling down my cheeks. Through the blur, I saw someone standing before me. I wiped my eyes. It was my beloved grandparents, holding hands, smiling. I really cried when I saw them. I thanked them for all they had done for me—for their encouragement and love, for feeding me, for nursing me as a child.

The tears were flowing, my voice was hoarse and cracked, but I was so happy they were there. They went away, but I knew they were still there, helping me, and that other spirits were watching over me.

Praying with my Pipe, hanging onto my Pipe like a man at sea clutching a branch for support, I was facing West when I heard the voice. It startled me, being so close. I jumped around looking for whoever it was. No one. It was the voice of the root.

Its words were: "I put this on men and it makes them better."

A conversational tone, simple, direct. No Charlton Heston booming drama, but a voice in the wilderness saying, "I put this on men and it makes them better."

Skin medicine! That's what I knew from the voice. Later that month, at the Sun Dance, I would use the root for the first time. It would heal a mother and her baby who were broken out with a bad rash.

Toward evening, Paula and Brian came up to see how I was faring. They brought with them some of the Giveaway presents for Uncle Bill, so that they would be blessed. The Altar and my sacrifice would accomplish the blessing. There was an expensive Hudson's Bay blanket in a heavy plastic pouch and some other things. Brian carried a bucket with hot coals and cedar. They cedared me with the blessing smoke. It refreshed me, strengthened me. Without a word, they went back down the hill.

I awoke the following dawn crazy with thirst. The plastic covering of the Hudson's Bay blanket was coated with a haze of dew. I licked it all over, getting a couple of drops, scarcely moistening my lips and tongue, thick and cracked in my mouth.

As the sun rose, I was facing East. The sun became the face of a beautiful girl, blindfolded. I remembered the prophecy.

I had lost track of time. Was this the first morning or the second? I sat on the now-trampled sage and gathered myself. Dwelling on my thirst, suffering, and getting more and more panicked weren't what I was here for. I was here to pray. The Spirit didn't respond to weakness, but to strength. Painfully, I stood up, faced West, and began to sing, holding onto my Pipe.

"*Wakantanka, onci malaye. Wani kta cha lecamun welo.*" ["Great Spirit, pity me. I want to live, so I do this."]

Each time I faced a new direction, I sang another song. Fierce energy and joy came over me in waves. The more tired I got, the harder I sang, danced, and cried, and the stronger I became. I went on for hours until my voice was gone, and only a croaking came from my stiff lips. Joy continued to wash over me. I looked at the trees and rejoiced. I rejoiced at the sight and sound of birds singing. Looking at this sacred Earth made me cry with joy. I rejoiced in my own worn-out body and in the energy Grandmother Earth kept sending me.

At last, toward evening, they came to get me. I was still singing. All they heard were gasps and grunts.

Back home, they put me in the Sweat Lodge. I sat in the back, looking out. The four sacred foods were lined up between the Altar mound and the door to the Lodge: cherry juice; *wasna*—made of dried meat, fat, and cherries; corn; and water in a mason jar. If my mouth could have watered, it would have. I was dying for that cherry juice.

Uncle Bill and the helpers entered the Sweat. Carefully, Uncle poured a little juice into the dipper and handed it to me. I drank, slowly. He gave me more, then passed the dish of *wasna*. I ate some. I could feel the nourishment surging through my body. Corn followed, then water, in the traditional order.

"*Ohan, Tunkska!* [Well, Nephew!] What have you to tell us?"

I told about the bee, my grandparents, the hummingbird, and the message of the root. My words were accompanied by a chorus of *Ho*s from the helpers.

"OK, Nephew, you done good. Now, you can smoke your *Cannunpa.*"

The fire keeper brought coals, and Uncle lit my Pipe for me. Gratefully, I took a deep drag, offering smoke to the six directions, giving my thanks. When I was finished Uncle spoke to the fire keeper.

"*Wana,* give us the rocks!"

At the dinner to break my fast after the Sweat, everything tasted wonderful. Uncle Bill was in top form, telling hilarious stories about other ceremonial events. A few of them were at my expense, like telling everyone that old man Crow Dog secretly called me Wic'as'ala Tanka—Little Big Man. The boys were making jokes about my cracked voice. But I also learned that Uncle had instructed some of them to sleep on the hill near me to keep guard. I'd never seen them at all. And Paula and the helpers told me how Eagle Feather had rooted them all out of bed before sunrise both mornings, so that he could make a Pipe ceremony to pray for my success.

After dinner, we had our Giveaway. Uncle got a few hundred dollars and the blanket. All the helpers got gifts. Uncle pointed at the clock on the kitchen wall. It was ten.

"Bedtime!" Eagle Feather announced.

I realized how totally fagged out I was. "I second the motion!"

We all got up, said our good nights, and headed for the sack. After two nights on the bare ground, the soft bed felt wonderful.

After breakfast next morning, I reminded Uncle Bill we still had a couple of days together, and what did he want to do?

"See our national capital," was his response.

Good night! Eagle Feather wanted to be a tourist. I said OK, we would go in my truck.

"Bring your camera," he said. "I wanna get a shot of me and the Capitol. Prove to them back home that I was here."

In Washington, Uncle Bill directed me in the exact placement of the camera. I photographed him standing with the Capitol dome over his head.

"Now what?" I wanted to know.

"Where's Washington's Monument?"

So I photographed him in front of the Washington Monument, and finally the White House.

"What do you want to see next, Uncle?"

"Take me to skid row!"

D.C. hardly had a skid row, I said. He wouldn't take no for an answer. He wanted the closest thing to a skid row, so I took him to Fourteenth Street.

We cruised north on Fourteenth, Uncle's big head swiveling back and forth, searching every face on the street. Finally, he was satisfied. He said we could go home.

"How come you wanted to see skid row, Uncle?"

He turned to me, his broad face serious. I have remembered his simple words ever since, and applied them in my own life.

"Sometimes, if you're lucky, that's where you can find the best prospects."

He was referring to the possibility of finding a human being willing and able to learn the spiritual path, and the good road. He said that even a bum had the potential of being a holy man, maybe even a better chance than a rich man, because the bum had run the gamut and bounced off the bottom, and he knew suffering. Years before, I'd had a painting studio on the Bowery, New York's skid row. I had experienced the truth of his words firsthand. I had talked with bums who were like saints.

A few days later, we embraced at the airport. He removed the big eagle feather from his hair, tied it into my hair, and said, "So long, see you at the Sun Dance."

For the first time in my life, I owned an eagle feather!

Fire Amble

Fire. Firelight. First light. Born out of darkness into the light, we feed the Fire in us and continue to look for the light. That's the true Peta owihankesni—*the Fire without end is in us.*

In the old stone farmhouse there were always fires to keep. My Grandpa kept saying, "Don't let the fire go out!" Fires in the kitchen, parlor, all the bedrooms. Late summer, we'd back up the old Model A to the sawbuck, jack up one rear wheel, replace the wheel with a pulley, and connect the two with a wide belt. The sawbuck would scream days on end as the three-foot whirling blade made our firewood for the coming winter. Dangerous, exciting, hard work, humping a hundred-pound log onto the cradle of the sawbuck, an elbow inches away from the whistling huge blade.

Winter nights Grandma would heat up flat stones, bricks, and flatirons on the woodstove, wrap them in towels, and stick them into our beds to warm them up for us. What a scuffle at sunrise to find a few embers to get the fires going, the temperature in the house around freezing!

A fire keeper gets to know in his guts what the fire means, physical and spiritual. One old medicine man had the honor name Petaga Yuha Mani [He Walks Carrying Coals of Fire]. That's what we're all doing, carrying the Fire for the coming generations.

CHAPTER SEVEN

Lowanpi:
The Ceremony in
the Cellar

Later that year, a few months after my Vision Quest, Eagle Feather called again.

"You been helpin' me with the cer'monies out here, now it's time you learned *Lowanpi.* How to make it yourself. How 'bout sendin' me a plane ticket?"

Lowanpi literally means "They sing." It is done in a darkened room like the *Yuwipi,* except the medicine man is not tied up. It is a ceremony used for healing, reconciliation, and other problems.

After checking with Paula, I made the travel arrangements for Uncle Bill. He arrived a few days later.

On the way home from the airport, Uncle started singing the Spirit Calling song in a low voice. The exhaust noises and rattles of my old truck made it almost impossible to hear him.

"D'ja get it?" Uncle asked.

I sang to him the few phrases I had heard over the roar of

the old Chevy. Uncle scowled, looking disgusted. I cringed, feeling that he was about to make one of his "slow learner" cracks. Instead, patiently, he began to sing the song again, this time in a louder voice.

"*Kola, ho uwa yelo he.*" ["Friends, I am calling you."] It was a song to the Powers of the six directions, asking for help.

During the forty-five-minute drive, I got most of it, Uncle singing the song repeatedly. He started in on the Pipe Filling song, but I begged him to hold off till we were out of the rattletrap truck.

At home Paula and I installed Eagle Feather in our bedroom and made up a bed for ourselves on the floor of Cody's room.

At the kitchen table over dinner, Uncle began discussing the place where we should hold the ceremonies. There would be two. The first one, he said, would be for me, and he would conduct it. The second one, I was to conduct. As is usual, the ceremony would require that we remove all the furniture, mirrors, and pictures from the room in which it was to be held. All windows and doors would have to be covered, so that no light would be visible.

We decided to use the cellar of our old stone farmhouse. It would be good, Eagle Feather said, because then we would be sitting on the earth, in total darkness.

Years later, after I had learned the ceremony, but before we had built the log ceremony house, we would hold the *Lowanpi* events in the living room. Everything in the room—couch, TV, chairs, paintings, and all other contents—was stored on the front porch till the sing was over. When we held two or more ceremonies, the stuff would stay outside for several days.

By ones and twos, the participating crew and helpers arrived. Richard and Ben, the sculptors, showed up. Brian hitched a ride in from upstate New York, and Beth drove in from Connecticut.

Just after the Sioux Nation Sun Dance the year before, a stranger named Steve had made his way to Eagle Feather's camp. At that time, only a few years after the Wounded Knee takeover, any non-Indian who showed up on the reservation was automatically suspect as an FBI agent. Some of the guys had asked me to find out who he was. Turned out he was a Yale student who was doing research for a paper on Indian religion. When Uncle Bill told him that I was from Maryland, Steve asked if he could visit me. He wound up bringing Kirk, who had assisted at the *Hanblecia.*

This time Kirk brought a few fellow Yalies with him. They were eager to help with the *Lowanpi.* They energetically cut and split wood for the fire, helped clean out the cellar, and did a dozen other things.

For the two days prior to the *Lowanpi* ceremonies, we made Sweat Lodge morning and night. Eagle Feather would hold court while the fire was heating the rocks. Seated on an old stump, he taught about the Indian religion. We sat at his feet or on wood chunks around him while he held forth on the sacredness of the Earth, how *Wakantanka* had invested his whole Creation with spirit. Not only human beings, but animals, trees—everything was imbued with spirit.

He talked about the Sweat Lodge Fire, *Peta owihankesni*— the everlasting Fire. We human beings pass that Fire on and on to the coming generations. We carry that Fire with us and in us, he said. When the Fire in us goes out, we go back to the Earth. That's why we have to pass that Fire on to our children, and teach them to take care of it and to be good caretakers of this sacred Earth.

Eagle Feather had directed me in building a Four-Generations fireplace. At the time, I had complained that a three-foot-diameter circle was too small to properly work the fire. He had said that if I faithfully performed the ceremony it would get bigger. It eventually got to be sixteen feet in diameter.

He also told me that if I did things right, the four sacred colors—black, red, yellow, white—would appear in the fireplace. They had, to my surprise. We sat around that fireplace as he taught about Grandfather Four Generations, which was what the fireplace represented.

"Elders told me that when ever'thing was done right, then the rock spirits, the water spirit, the Earth spirit, an' the Four Generations fire spirit would keep you alive long enough so you'd see your Four Generations. You'd be so healthy you'd live to see your great-grandchildren. That's four generations from you."

He shook out a Salem Light from a crumpled pack and lit up.

"The *Inipi* or *Inikaga* means 'the thing that makes us live,' or 'breath of life.' It's devoted to the promotion of life an' health. But then, ever' one of our cer'monies is devoted to the same thing, 'specially the sacred Pipe. That's why she came an' gave us this greatest gift, because *Tunkasila*—Grandfather Above—wanted us to live an' be healthy."

Uncle Bill was referring to Ptehincala ska winyan—the White Buffalo Calf Woman—who had come centuries ago and given the Sioux people the Pipe, a sacred gift from the Creator.

"*Cannunpa* [the Pipe]. That is the center of our religion, an' the center of ever'thing for most Indian people. But! We had this," he waved his hand at the fire and the Sweat Lodge, "long before we had the Pipe! This was the old-time way we had of preservin' an' promotin' life an' health."

He paused, staring hard at each of us. He took a deep breath, as if he were going to say something dramatic. Instead, in a voice surprisingly little for such a big man, he reverently said, "An' we still have it because of our elders like Black Elk, in spite of how hard the gov'mint's tried to take it away."

He sat back, took a final drag on his cigarette, looked sharply at the Yalies, and said, "*Han!* [Yes!] Mebbe you didn't know that, huh? In this land of religious freedom, Indians is the only ones forbidden to practice our God-given religion."

He surveyed the shock and disbelief registered on the young faces around him.

"*Ohan!* Technically speakin', you're doin' somethin'—*I'm* doin' somethin' illegal right now. Yes! Back home, if I want to practice my religion, I'm s'posed t' get permission from the gov'mint's agent on the reservation. You didn't know that now, did you?"

He glanced at the fire again, checking to see if the rocks were ready. Rubbing his big-nosed rugged face with a large hand, he reflected on the faces of the Ivy Leaguers. Richard, Brian, and I knew what he was talking about.

"We had to practice our religion in secret. When we wanted to hold a big cer'mony, like Sun Dance, we had to hide out in the badlands. You could be thrown in jail for makin' any of the cer'monies—*Inipi,* Sun Dance, 'specially the prayer cer'mony we call *Lowanpi*—the one we're doin' here later on.

In a bittersweet tone he continued.

"Did you know there's a bill in Congress right now aimin' to give us our religious freedom? Isn't it somethin'? They had to make up a whole new bill declarin' us Indians could worship God our own way! It's called the 1978 Native American Freedom of Religion Act. Henry's got a copy 'cause I give it to him. I think it's gonna pass, or maybe passed already."

It did pass, and since 1979 Indians have had the legal right, for the first time in our nation's history, to practice their religion.*

I turned to Uncle Bill, asking him if it was time to fill the

---

*Bill Eagle Feather and others had started openly defying the government ban on practicing their religion ten or more years before the 1978 Native American Freedom of Religion Act was passed. Prior to passage of the bill, they were subject to arrest for Sun Dancing or performing other religious ceremonies such as the *Lowanpi* and *Yuwipi.*

Pipe. He grunted, got up, took his Pipe bag from the Altar mound, removed his shoes, and entered the Sweat Lodge.

"Bring me some hot coals an' that *Wac'anga* [sweetgrass]."

I kneeled at the low entrance of the Sweat and lighted the sweetgrass with the coals Richard brought on a shovel. Eagle Feather removed the stone Pipe and its stem from the Pipe bag. Carefully, he incensed them, licked the stem, and fitted stem and Pipe together. He incensed the whole Pipe, laid it reverently on a bed of sage he had prepared, and took the first pinch of tobacco from the Pipe bag. Passing the tobacco through the sweetgrass smoke, he offered it to the Powers of the West.

"*Ho Tunkasila Wiyohpeyata, Wakinyan oyate, anpetu kin le ho ye wayinkte.*" ["O Grandfather West, Winged Nation, today I am going to send you my voice. Hear me all over this land. With my relatives, I want to live in health. That's why I do this."]

He repeated the offering to the other three directions, then Above and Below. When he finished, he incensed the filled Pipe, and placed it in the center of the Sweat Lodge. Grunting, he squeezed out through the little door of the Lodge and stood up, putting his Pipe bag back on the mound.

"OK. Time to fry some skin. Let's get ready."

He took off his shirt. The women went to the little house near the Sweat to change into house dresses or large beach towels. The men, behind the Lodge, took off their clothes and wrapped big towels around themselves, except for Brian, who was the doorkeeper. Uncle reentered the Sweat Lodge, naked except for the towel hanging from his big belly.

"*Hiyupo!*" ["Come on in!"]

I entered last, sitting across the doorway from him, acting as his helper. He handed me the sweetgrass braid for the incensing and hollered for Brian to bring hot coals. Uncle gave the cedar bag to Richard and told him to put the herb on the first six rocks.

As the glowing rocks came through the door, Eagle Feather silently touched them with the mouthpiece of the Pipe. After the first six, he handed the Pipe out to Brian, who put it on the Altar mound. After the rest of the rocks were in place, Brian handed in the bucket of water. Uncle and I grasped the bail and touched the bottom of the bucket to the hot rocks. Brian closed the door flap and tucked the blankets in. Except for the incandescent rocks, the Lodge was dark.

In a low voice Eagle Feather welcomed everyone and began his first song.

"Kola, lecel ecun woy!" ["Friend, do it this way. If you do so, whatever you pray for will come to you!"]

It was a good, hot one. Everyone made beautiful prayers. At the end, Uncle asked the spirits to bless the food and all the participants.

After dressing, we had a big dinner in the farmhouse kitchen.

"Now, tomorrow we'll go out an' cut your sticks." Eagle Feather briefed us on our final preparations as he sipped his second coffee.

The *Lowanpi* ceremony is sometimes referred to as a "Five Stick Ceremony" because of the five tall forked wands that carry the cloth offerings and delineate the central Altar—one for each direction and one for the center, which also denotes the Above and Below.

"An' we need five coffee cans, an' that special sacred earth to fill 'em. Can you get that dirt?"

I had already scouted out the area for mole hills. No problem, I told him.

"Pala"—his way of saying *Paula*—"we need a blanket. Can you go out an' get Henry a blanket?"

Paula said we had plenty of blankets. That wouldn't do, Uncle said. It had to be a new blanket.

He never said what the blanket was for. Unknown to me,

that blanket was to become my ceremonial robe. Our financial situation was always in a state of crisis, especially so since I had become Uncle Bill's student. The Giveaways and plane tickets meant that even emergency repairs to the house were put on hold. Holes were covered up with plastic bags; the cracked, leaking toilet was actually patched with chewing gum. The spiritual education Paula and I were receiving made it worthwhile.

Not knowing that this blanket would be with me for the rest of my life, Paula went to K-Mart and bought what our few dollars could afford, a cheap polyester blanket.

"Oh," said Uncle when he saw the blanket. Never a word of explanation.

That was his way. His favorite saying, "God gave you a brain, you figure it out," was an indication of how much each student should rely on his own active intelligent search for the meaning inherent in Eagle Feather's teaching, and in the spirits' teaching. I should have had the wit to figure out the purpose for the blanket.

"Oh," he said, "this is the blanket you will use. Gimme a piece of paper."

He sketched out the designs that should go in each corner of the blanket. I was to cut them out of colored felt. Paula would sew them on. Thunderstruck, I realized then what the blanket was to be—the robe I would wear or use when I made my own ceremonies. "Why didn't you tell me?" I asked.

"No," he responded. "This is your blanket. Future times, it'll mean somethin' to you. Now, cut out them signs an' get 'em sewn on there!"

To Uncle Bill, everything was a lesson. My ignorance of the moment would carry a meaning in the years ahead. He was right. The blanket still reminds me to pay careful attention to words and situations.

When the blanket was finished, we went out in the woods,

cut five slender forked sticks, and brought them back to the house.

"OK, now, take them sticks an' the cans an' paint 'em." He instructed me how to paint the sticks and cans with the four sacred colors. When they were dry, Uncle told me to fill the cans with earth and take everything into the cellar.

Brian and the others had cleaned and prepared the cellar. The small windows were blacked out, the floor swept, and cushions and blankets placed against the walls for people to sit on. I put the cans and sticks in the center of the cleared space.

Eagle Feather announced it was time to practice our singing. I had made two small hand drums of rawhide buckskin and wood. We all sat down on the cushions, and Uncle Bill began teaching us four songs, the minimum needed to put on the ceremony. Over and over we sang the Pipe Filling song, the Spirit Calling song, the Pipe song, and the Quitting song. Years later, many other songs were sung in these ceremonies, as is usually done—the Prayer song, the Rock song, the Thunder song, and others.

The drums and our voices made an awesome tumultuous sound within the rough stone walls of the little cellar. Finally, Uncle said we had it down good enough to call the spirits. We went upstairs for sandwiches and coffee, and to finish our tobacco ties.

Making those 405 prayer ties was tedious work. Later, Paula and I would become so proficient that we would complete a hundred an hour—which still meant more than four hours to make the one string of ties to surround the Altar. But that day it took even longer than that. Richard, Brian, and the others made additional short strings of ties, prayer offerings that the ceremonies would go well.

Toward evening, everything was ready, including the ceremony food: *wohanpi,* or soup, *wojapi,* or fruit pudding, fry bread, *ceyaka,* or mint tea, coffee, and cake. Humble, healthy, and traditional food. All would be in the cellar with us, to be consumed at the end of the ceremony as the final act of the *Lowanpi*.

While the others were out back preparing the Sweat Lodge, the usual preliminary to the ceremonies, Uncle Bill took me into the cellar. We sat down on the cushions, our backs resting against the wall. He took out his Salem Lights, offered me one, and we lit up.

"*Tunkska*," he began. "Tonight I'm gonna be in the middle. You got to pay attention, 'cause tomorrow night you're gonna be out there, an' I an' the kids are gonna be singin' for you!"

Although I had been in many *Lowanpi* ceremonies on the reservation, I was very nervous about the process, and he read my mind.

"Don't you worry about a thing. All you gotta do is keep your wits about you, remember the order of things, an' let me an' the spirits take care of everything. I'll be right there t' back you up. Now, your blanket'll be spread out on the floor in the center, the four sticks with the cloth offerings'll be in the corners of the blanket, an' the fifth stick—the one painted red an' black—it'll be right in front of you between the West stick an' the North stick. That eagle feather'll be tied to the top."

He and Paula had made a special amulet for me. It looked like a miniature dream catcher or spirit catcher, sort of a spider web in a three-inch hoop of peeled willow. Designating that, he said, "You'll tie this other thing to the middle of the stick."

He pulled a rawhide rattle, referred to as a gourd, out of his medicine bundle. "You got a rattle already, a good one, an' I'm givin' you this." Ceremoniously, he handed it to me, an out-and-out gift of one of his sacred objects. I thanked him, overwhelmed by his generosity, and asked him what I should do with the gourds.

"Don't you worry. When the spirits come in, why, you'll know what to do. They'll take care of everything."

He brushed off my nervous questioning, stubbed out his cigarette, and continued.

"Now, between you an' the center stick you're gonna set up an earth Altar, just like you seen me do it before."

This is a small flattened mound of dry earth, in which are scribed certain marks, usually making a face, relating to the ceremony. It is an homage and an appeal to Mother Earth.

"The rattles'll be to the left of it, the bowl of water to the right."

The water was sanctified by the ceremony and communally drunk by all participants at the end.

"First thing you'll do is get me, your helper, to smudge ever'one in the room with sweetgrass. We'll need a bucket of hot coals from the Sweat fire for that. Then, you're gonna fill the Pipe. I'll drop cedar in the bucket an' you'll smudge ever pinch of tobacco before offerin' it to the directions. Make prayers as you're doin' that. We'll be singin' the Pipe Fillin' song. Then, when you're finished, maybe you oughta stand up an' tell the people how come you're out there in the center."

He was referring to the part of the ceremony known as *Hanbloglaka,* or the telling of one's vision, a kind of validation of one's right to perform the ceremony. Eagle Feather suggested I talk about how, years before, the eagle had come to me and brushed my face with his wings. I had dreamed of that time again in Uncle Moses' house during Uncle Bill's funeral.

"Now, the lights'll go out an' we'll start singin' the Spirit Calling song. We'll keep it up till the spirits come in an' you tell us to quit. Don't be afraid of anything. They'll check you out, an' check out the whole place, people an' all."

The crew knocked on the cellar door and entered, saying that the rocks were hot. It was time to go out to have our purification Lodge. The students who were new to this were concerned that they wouldn't be able to remember the words to the songs. Sitting down on the cushions, some pulled out rumpled sheets of notepaper, asking Eagle Feather whether they had the lyrics right. Uncle Bill's face cracked into a Puckish grin.

"I suppose you wrote them songs down in firefly's ink, so you can see 'em when the lights are all out, huh? Put that stuff away. Don't worry, you got them songs down good!"

Looking a little foolish, they stuck the notes back in their pockets. Grunting, Uncle got to his feet.

"Tell you what. We'll just practice 'em once more in the Sweat. Now, get your towels an' let's go *Inikaga* [have a Sweat Lodge ceremony]!"

In the clear evening's afterglow, he led the way back to the Sweat Lodge. We crawled in, each one saying the words "All my relations." Kirk brought in the glowing rocks. This was a quick one, a one-water Sweat. A regular ceremony is a four-water Sweat—that is, water is poured over the rocks four times, with the door being opened between each round. During Sun Dance and other ceremonies, where the Sweat Lodge is a preliminary purification to the greater ceremony, one water is poured.

When we came back to the cellar, Paula and some of the helpers brought the ceremony food down from the kitchen and, as is done in these ceremonies, laid it out on the floor away from the central area.

Uncle Bill began laying out his Altar, positioning the painted coffee cans with their staffs in the corners of a six-foot square in the center of the room. He tied an eagle feather to the top of the fifth staff and stuck it in the can positioned between the West and North cans. People settled themselves into the cushions around the edges of the room, quietly observing his actions. Paula gave him the bowl of water, and he put it next to the North can.

He began pulling the sacred objects out of his *wopiye*, or medicine bag: his Pipe, rattles, eagle fan, and earth Altar. Carefully, reverently, he set up the Altar. Just inside the central can and staff, he poured out the special earth onto a small piece of cloth. I passed him my drum and, using the drum-head, he flattened the earth mound into a small disk six inches in diameter.

Paula sat in front of him on the other side of the central staff. She would be the Pipe holder. A woman holds the Pipe in these ceremonies, in honor of the White Buffalo Calf Woman, who originally brought the sacred Pipe to the Indian people.

"OK, *Tunkska*, start rollin' those tobacco ties around the Altar."

I began with the West, the black staff and can, slowly unrolling the big ball of ties past the central can toward the North, the red can. When I had reached the East, the yellow can, Uncle ordered me to stop.

"Don't close me in here yet. Wait'll I fill the Pipe."

I went outside, got the bucket of hot coals from the Sweat fire, and returned to squat down next to him just outside the Altar, holding the cedar bag. Ceremonially, he put his Pipe together, and reached into his Pipe bag for a pinch of tobacco.

"*Wana, Hante!*" ["Now, cedar!"]

I dropped a handful of cedar into the bucket. Instantly the fragrant smoke rose into the room. Eagle Feather incensed the tobacco and placed it in the Pipe.

When the Pipe was filled, he stood up to pray to the six directions.

"*Wana, Cannunpa opagi olowan.*" ["Now, let's have the Pipe Filling song."]

The lights were dimmed. Hesitantly, the novices began to sing.

"*Kola, lecel ecun woy.*" ["Friend do it this way. If you do so, whatever you pray for will come to you."]

We got stronger. By the time Eagle Feather was finished, we were sounding really good. Uncle Bill sat down. Solemnly, he handed the Pipe to Paula. She grasped it, the stone bowl in her left hand, the stem in her right, pointed away from her toward the space over the Altar. The lights came on again. I got up and resumed rolling the ties around the Altar. When I got to Paula I put down the ball of ties, carefully taking the Pipe from her. Keeping it pointed in the same direction, East, I passed between Paula and the center stick. I handed the Pipe back to my wife, knelt down, and resumed rolling the ties toward the red can.

Uncle Bill continued his teaching. "See that? There's a reason why he's doin' that maneuver. You hafta understand that *nothin'* comes before the filled Pipe! That *Cannunpa* is sacred. When it's filled, it's powerful, like a loaded gun. No one should walk in front of it. So that's why Henry takes it from the Pipe holder, passes in front of her, an' then hands it back. That's showin' respect for our most holy. All right, Nephew, finish puttin' out them ties."

Eagle Feather sat inside the Altar facing the center stick, the earth Altar, and Paula, as I continued with the ties. I had to take the Pipe from Paula twice more before I came to the end of the string. I picked up my drum and sat down on the cushions against the north wall. Uncle Bill spoke.

"Now, before we douse the lights, I want ever'body to just look at what we've made. Look at this Altar, the flags, look at all these offerings, the eagle feather—ever'thing! Its just beautiful. Bee-yoo-tee-ful! Perfect in every way! That's the way the spirits like to see things done. Just right." He praised all of us present for our part in making things turn out so well.

We gazed at the Altar, and the old man who sat in it. Several craned or half-stood to see every part of it. Beautiful. It was mysterious, somehow exotic, a supplication and offering to the Powers of the World and the Great Spirit. Each of us belonged there; we wore that Altar, and it wore us. We were all relations, and Uncle Bill was helping us become good relations to the spirit world. We looked at one another, seeing and feeling happiness, peace, and harmony. Eagle Feather cleared his throat.

"Time to begin. Douse the lights."

Brian pulled the main switch for the house. By the light of a small flashlight, he found his way back to his seat, then turned off that light. In total velvety darkness we sat in silence, the warm earthy smell of the cellar surrounding us.

In a low voice, Eagle Feather began by saying "All my relations" and welcoming us to this holy and mysterious ceremony. He asked us not to touch the spirits when they came, but to greet them by saying, "*Ho, Tunkasila* [Hello, Grandfather]" and to treat them with respect.

He was silent for a few moments, letting us get used to the feeling and the blind emptiness of the room.

"This darkness is to remind us that we're ignorant an' hafta always remember to seek an' pray for the light. *Ho, hecetu welo.* [So be it.] That's what the elders taught me. Tonight we come here to ask the spirits for help so that Henry can go on an' help people in a ceremonial way. So, let's sing the Spirit Calling song."

Richard and I began tapping our drums in a ragged rhythm. We found the beat and, in unison, began the song. The others joined us.

"*Kola, ho uwa yelo he.*" ["Friends, I am calling you."]

We sang to the West, "*Wiyohpeyata, sunka wakan oyate.*"— ["Toward the West, a Horse Nation, we need your help."]

We sang to the four directions, to the Above and Below, repeating the song over and over, the roar of the drums and voices seeming to shatter the blackness of the little room. There suddenly appeared a little light near the ceiling.

"*Ho, Tunkasila!*" we all hollered.

The little light moved rapidly about. A shower of little lights appeared, sparks flying through the air all over the room. They gathered around the drums. Each time I hit the drum with the stick, they followed the stick, making a trail of light between the drumhead and the moving stick. We kept on singing, stronger and stronger. The lights moved over to the earth Altar in front of Uncle Bill and seemed to sit on the Pipe in Paula's hands. We heard Uncle talking to them. They went to the rattles, and the rattles began to move, rolling on the floor, flying through the air, invisible in the darkness. Cody, sitting on the opposite side of the room from me, shouted out.

"Hey, he hit me on the head!"

Nervous laughter. The rattles were striking, tapping, stroking each person in the room as the spirits investigated the crowd. Different people cried out as this happened, some scared or startled.

"Ho, Tunkasila! Hey! Whoa!"

The spirits had arrived. We stopped singing, the silence broken only by the sound of the rattles moving around the room. The spirits gathered around the earth Altar in front of Uncle Bill. He seemed to be talking to them, in a strange language. Then he interpreted their messages to us. They were well pleased by what they had found. They wanted to hear our prayers.

"Now, you guys don't know the Four Directions song, so I an' Henry will sing it. What it says is, 'Look over there to the West, your Grandfather is sittin' there, lookin' this way. Pray to him, he's sittin' there lookin' this way.' Then we sing to the North, East, South, Above, an' Below. But I want ever'body to join in on the chorus. *Cekiya yo, cekiya yo.* It means pray to him—or her. OK, drums, hit it."

Richard and I began drumming. In a powerful voice Uncle Bill began to sing. I joined in.

"Wiyohpeyata, etun wan yo, nitunkasila ahitunwan yankelo, cekiya yo, cekiya yo."

When we sang to the North, a few voices hesitantly joined in on the chorus. Gradually, everybody was helping out with the singing. When we finished, there was dead silence for a few moments, then Paula began the prayers. She finished with "All my relations." The person to her left began to pray.

The prayers went clockwise around the Altar, each person finishing with "All my relations." A beautiful, moving experience it was to hear young people pouring out their hearts, asking for help for sick relatives, or friends in difficulty, and praying for me, for Uncle Bill, and for all our relations.

Eagle Feather finished the round.

"*Ho Tunkasila Wakantanka* [Oh Grandfather Great Mystery], hear the voices of us, your children. These humble prayers are so beautiful. I know you are listening, and will give them their answers. All my relations."

During the prayers, the spirits had been silent, but we could feel them like a wind blowing in the now stuffy room.

Uncle asked for the Pipe song. When we began, once more we could see and hear them.

"*Le miye ca, Cannunpa yuha.*" ["This is me, holding this Pipe. I do this because I want to live in health with my relatives."]

Finally, Uncle Bill asked for the Quitting, or Spirits Leaving, song. He said that the spirits were hungry and wanted us to get to the food so they could have some. A wave of giggles went round.

Earlier, while we were practicing the singing in the afternoon, Eagle Feather had given me and the others a loose narrative translation of the song, which went like this: "Well, the spirits are standin' out there, an' they are talkin'. They are happy with all the prayers an' vows they heard. They are sayin', 'Grandfather, your influence is everywhere in these gifts.'"

We were happy ourselves as we began the song.

"*Hotaniyan kin nazin pelo he. Tunkasila, ta wokunze ca lena cicu welo he.*"

As the drums tapped their last beats, Uncle spoke up.

"*Wowas'telo! Ho hecetu welo!* [Really good! So be it!] OK, Brine"—his way of saying *Brian*—"let's have the lights."

The sixty-watt bulb blinded us. We blinked, squinted, and

peered around the room. Uncle Bill was still sitting the same way he had been when the lights went out an hour and a half ago. All the ties were neatly rolled into a ball sitting next to the earth Altar. The flags had been twined together and were lying in Paula's lap. When she picked them up, we saw that they resembled a human figure, a doll made of the four colors and tobacco.

Paula handed the Pipe to Eagle Feather. He lit it, offered it to the six directions, and passed it back to her. Paula smoked, said "All my relations," and passed the Pipe to her left. The Pipe went around the room, each person smoking and saying "All my relations" before passing it on. It came back to Uncle Bill, who finished it, raised it devotedly to the sky, said, "All my relations," and took the Pipe apart, putting it into the Pipe bag.

Next, he took the big red-enameled copper bowl of water and passed it to Paula.* She received it ceremonially, drank, and passed it on, saying, "All my relations." The bowl in turn went around. When Uncle Bill got it back, he made a humorous crack about how we had left him half a gallon to drink. He took his time, got it all down, and began to disassemble the Altar, putting the sacred objects back into his medicine suitcase.

The food was brought out to the center, and the youngest men began to serve everyone, first preparing a small dish for the spirits, which was placed outside under the moonlit sky.

During the sharing of the food, there was much joviality and laughter as we spoke of our personal experiences with the spirits during the ceremony. Cody wanted to know who the guy was that kept bothering him. Uncle told him that it was Circle Elk, one of his (Bill's) spirits.

The last of the food was eaten, the coffee and mint tea were all gone. Uncle spoke up.

---

*This red-enameled bowl has been used for more than twenty years' worth of ceremonies.

"Time to finish this cer'mony an' get to bed. Ever'body stand up."

Starting left of the door, each person said in turn, "All my relations." The ceremony was finished. The door was opened, letting in the cool night air.

By next evening, I was in a cold sweat. It was my turn to be out in the center and, boy, did I have a case of the butterflies. Once I began to concentrate on setting up my Altar, I calmed down a bit. I was awkward and crude, compared to Eagle Feather, but he kept encouraging me. He would say that I should remember that I was a beginner and bound to make mistakes. Everything was going to be just fine, he said. Having him there to check on my every move gave me confidence. Still, I was sweating with nervous anxiety.

My holy yellow blanket was down; the cans, sticks, and offerings were all set up; and everyone was settled in their places. I was ready to begin. At that point Eagle Feather removed his shirt. When a medicine man conducts a ceremony, he normally removes shoes and shirt as an act of humbleness. I thought that was what Uncle had in mind, but it was something else. He produced a razor blade and a needle.

"*Wana, Tunkska.* You're gonna take six flesh from me!"

He was offering his own flesh that I might do well! I had given flesh and seen the flesh offering ceremony many times. Although I had done an eagle-feather piercing for a brother Sun Dancer in 1976, I had never cut another's body before. I was shaking as I handed Uncle my Pipe to hold during the cutting. I felt small, humble, unequal to this test.

He stood on the eastern edge of my blanket, facing the West, the earth Altar, and the center stick with its eagle feather. I stuck the needle in his upper arm, pulled up, and sliced off a bit of flesh. Blood began to run down his arm. The second was harder. I sawed the blade back and forth, trying to sever the flesh. Never a wince or flinch from the old man. I sawed away on the third. Uncle spoke up.

"These guys that saw like they was workin' on a hunk of wood."

Sympathetic laughter. The last three pieces, I took with one swipe of the razor. As I was taught, I took a handful of sacred earth, spat on the bleeding wounds, and rubbed the dirt in, stopping the flow. The drops of blood Bill Eagle Feather shed for me are to this day visible on my ceremony blanket.

The *Lowanpi* went as Uncle had predicted. Once the lights were out and the Spirit Calling song had begun, I became calm. Later, everyone remarked on how fast the spirits had come in. They came to me, helped me, told me things. It was like having my ancestors whisper in my ears. Sometimes they spoke in tiny voices, sometimes it was as if they put thoughts in my head, a kind of ESP.

During ceremonies in later years, I would at some point realize they were telling me things to tell the people. Sometimes I wouldn't know what I was saying during the ceremony or couldn't recall it afterward. As I write about it, I find that I still can't really explain it.

When the lights went on, the tobacco ties were in a ball in front of me. The cloth offerings had been made into a doll. Someone got that doll following the ceremony, but I forget who.

As we were eating, to my astonishment, I heard Uncle Bill say that I was a medicine man. I had a hard time believing it. I felt I had a long way to go, and felt that way for a long time after his death. I was flattered and grateful for his confidence in me. He knew a lot more than I did, or ever will. I felt the announcement was premature, although until his death he treated me as if it were true.

What I am is a helper.

The next day, after everyone had left, Uncle Bill announced he wanted to see Baltimore. I trucked him around to all the attractions, including the eighteenth-century battleship, the *Constellation*. The chief petty officer took us on a tour, captain's cabin and all. He pointed out many wrought-iron hooks in the ceiling between decks, saying that 250 sailors had slung their hammocks there. Uncle Bill had a technical question.

"Say, where'd all those guys go to take a shit?"

The CPO's eyes lit up. He took us above to the main deck and forward to the huge bowsprit. He enthusiastically explained the origin of the navy term *head*.

"Imagine if you can, sir, having to walk those braces out to the end of that spar, dropping your pants, and taking a dump in a forty-knot gale!"

Uncle was impressed with the novel way the *wasicun*, or white man, had of taking care of business.

We left the ship. Where next? Uncle wanted to see skid row. I took him to East Baltimore Street, known as "the Block." No bums, lots of hookers and honky-tonks. Uncle's gray braids flew as he swiveled his big head around, taking it all in.

"What's all these bookstores?"

Before I could explain, he headed for one. When the clerk told him about the movies to be seen in the little booths, he pushed me ahead of him into the tiny space and dropped a quarter in the slot. Guys doing it to girls, black guys doing it to white girls, three guys doing it to one girl, guys doing it to guys. We both got a bit steamed up. But what's Uncle Bill doing during the whole performance? Giving the spiritual explanation of the action!

A medicine man is a holy man, but he is a man first. John Fire Lame Deer, one of Uncle Bill's teachers, used to say, "They don't pay me to be good, they pay me because I got the power!" As we came out of the store onto the street, Uncle Bill said, "OK, Henry, now let's find a real one! Which ones are the ones that do it?"

I said the ones with the short skirts. His head swung

around as he surveyed the possibilities. Oh. His face registered disappointment. I guessed that the girls were a little too raunchy for him. Eyebrows up, shaking his head, he spoke.

"Well, Henry, we best be gettin' home."

He sighed as I moved the truck out into traffic. In an hour, we were sitting in the kitchen, eating Paula's good food.

The next day, as we said goodbye at the airport, he laid his big hand on my head.

"*Tunkasila niye aya was'tepo.* [God bless you an' your family], Henry. Thanks for ever'thing. Be seein' you at the Sun Dance."

"God bless you, Uncle."

Amble at Death's Door

People do get up off their deathbeds and go on with their lives. Uncle Bill did it a couple of times.

When he finally went, it wasn't from a deathbed. He was in action, crawling out of a Sweat Lodge. Way to go! I want to do it that way.

There was an old Rosebud guy who Sun Danced every year. Up in his seventies, he kept right on dancing. Every year he prayed and prayed to die while he was dancing in that Sacred Hoop. This made all the Sun Dance leaders very nervous. Because if he did, they would have a terrible time explaining it to the Bureau of Indian Affairs agent. This was in the days before the Freedom of Religion Act was passed by Congress.

I saw my dad, my mom, Turkey, and others die in hospital beds. Not for me. Dancing, praying, helping others, I want to walk through that door. Today, or any other day, is a good day to die! Just so's I can do it in action, like Uncle Bill.

CHAPTER EIGHT

Dying:
He Sees the Ghost
Diggers

Winter seemed to hang on during March of 1978. It would snow, then get bright and warm, then snow again. There were seventeen little lambs already born and more coming. I was running out of hay, and the pasture hadn't started to show green yet.

One morning just after breakfast, the phone rang. It was Aunt Hazel calling from the reservation, sixteen hundred miles away.

"You better get out here quick. He's in the hospital. They say he's dying, that he don't have long to go. He's calling for you and Paula."

"Oh, shit!" I thought. I said a quiet prayer for my Uncle Bill, asking that I be allowed to see him before he went.

"How are the roads out there, Aunt Hazel? What do you hear?"

She put her hand over the phone. I could hear her muffled voice talking to someone else.

"Grandson says 20 is clear to Sioux City. Amos says the Interstates are clear—80 and 90. The tribe has the roads here pretty clean. Nephew, get out here soon's you can!"

Paula's face was pale as I told her the news. "Start getting ready, honey. I'll call the school and tell them I'm coming for Cody. Get out the sleeping bags and quilts. We'll probably be staying down in camp in the log house. It'll be cold!"

The last time I'd been there in March it was twenty below zero during the nights.

After I called the school, I made motel reservations in Madison and in Sioux Falls. By myself, I was used to doing the sixteen hundred miles in one shot, thirty-two hours straight through. With the family, we had to make a few stops.

By daybreak the next morning, we were a hundred miles on our way. We pulled into the motel in Madison, Wisconsin, at sunset. All through Ohio, Indiana, and Illinois, we had passed many cars off the road and eighteen-wheeler after eighteen-wheeler on their sides, in the ditches, and sometimes way off in the bushes. The roads were icy, and a powerful north wind was blowing.

But the ugly old green Dodge station wagon had hauled us through, at least the first lap. I had the feeling it was going to be an easy trip.

The next day proved me wrong. Up before dawn, flapjacks and coffee under our belts, Cody asleep in the back, we passed through the beautiful countryside around Wisconsin Dells on Interstate 90. The driving was easier through the trees, which broke the wind's force. We drove across the Mississippi and up the long incline to Minnesota's flatlands. We stopped at a good diner for lunch around Albert Lea. I figured we were ahead of schedule, so we took our time.

Back in the car in the parking lot, Cody went off to sleep, Paula started to snooze, so I figured a ten-minute catnap would do me good. I woke up a half-hour later. The weather had changed. A warm Chinook wind was blowing. It was midafternoon but already starting to get dark. Heavy clouds were blowing in from the southwest. It was above freezing, and mist was beginning to blow off the snowbanks lining the highway.

"Feet, do yo' stuff!" I said to myself, and tromped on the gas. I didn't want to get caught out if the weather was going to turn foggy.

The old 318 engine was wailing, and we were doing seventy-five on a highway still slick in spots.

The fog began to get thicker. I slowed down to sixty. As it got darker, visibility got worse and worse. I had to go slower—fifty, then forty. We had told the motel in Sioux Falls we'd be in at seven that evening.

We were still eighty miles east of South Dakota at seven. Visibility had dropped to zero. Even with the window open and my head out, looking straight down at the road, I couldn't see the white line. I moved over into the passing lane because the line on its left margin was yellow. I could see that. I didn't dare travel any faster than ten miles an hour.

I was talking to an eighteen-wheel truck driver on the CB radio. He was only a quarter-mile in front of me, also traveling at ten miles per hour. I never saw him. Once in a while, I could spot a mile marker and I would radio him my position.

He would radio back, "I just passed that marker—a couple minutes ago, old buddy!"

"Well, we got to be only a couple hundred yards apart. Can you see my lights?" I would ask him.

"Nary a glimmer, driver," was his reply.

We went on like that hour after hour, totally isolated from the world except for the disembodied voice on the CB. It was some of the hairiest driving I had ever done.

We finally saw the lights of Sioux Falls and got to the motel at ten o'clock. I had a miserable stiff neck and a headache after fifteen hours of driving.

"If it's like this in the morning, we're sleeping in!" I announced. But it was bright and sunny the next day, and we took off on the last leg of the trip.

Around three in the afternoon, we pulled into the Indian Health Service hospital parking lot on the reservation. They must have been on the lookout for us, because Aunt Hazel, Delores, and Chunzila all greeted us as we came in the main entrance.

Aunt Hazel said, "He's not good. Be prepared. He's got a lot of wires and needles in him." They wouldn't let Cody into Uncle Bill's room, so Chunzila stayed outside with him. I walked into the room with Paula and Aunt Hazel.

Uncle Bill's large frame lay inert, covered by a sheet, on the old metal cot. On his feet, he was an imposing figure. In the hospital bed he looked old and pitiful. His eyes were closed, his head turned to the window. There were four EKG electrodes on his body and an IV needle stuck in each arm. His arms were stretched out, palms up, on either side of him. It was as if he were imploring the One Above for help with his outstretched arms.

Aunt Hazel busily moved to his side and jiggled the bed.

"Bill, Bill! They came! Look who's here!"

Uncle slowly opened his eyes, turning his broad face toward us. He was haggard and pale, but when he recognized us, an amazing transformation took place.

"Oh, you made it. Reeeally good! Where's Cody? Did you bring him?"

Instantly, he became lively, trying to hitch himself up in bed to a sitting position. Later they told us that he hadn't talked for days, and it was like a miracle. We reassured him that Cody was with us. He got even livelier.

"Hazel, gimme my clothes. I can't stand this no more. We're going home!" Aunt Hazel told him that Delores had taken his clothes home to wash them.

"Well, get Daughter in here! Tell her to bring me my pants!"

Delores was out in the hall wringing her hands when I went out to tell her. She had heard her dad speak. In a nervous whisper, she told me that she had wrecked his favorite car, the blue '62 Ford. She was too scared to tell him.

"What am I gonna do? He'll kill me! He didn't want nobody drivin' his car, but mine broke an' I had to use his to get food."

I could hear Auntie telling Bill that he was too weak to leave—the doctor wanted him to stay a couple more days.

"Well, you tell Delores to bring my pants tomorrow, or I'm walkin' out of here in this fool gown! Get Henry back in here, I wanna talk to him."

I walked back into the room.

Bill said, "Hazel, you an' Pala go talk to Delores about tomorrow."

When they left he whispered hoarsely to me, "I gotta get out of here. I seen them out there waitin' for me!"

He nodded toward the window. Out the window a bare prairie hillside rose toward the horizon. The hill was only about three hundred feet away, level with the hospital's second story window.

"Uncle, who? Who did you see?"

He whispered, "Spirits! Ghost women, digging *tinpsila!* Get me outta here!"

He was referring to the prairie turnips that still grow out there, though the range stock gets most of them. In the old days, the women would go out from the camp to dig them for soup or to dry for wintertime. Uncle Bill was scared they had come for him and were hanging around on the hillside waiting for him to die. I promised him we would take him home the next day.

Leaving the hospital, we followed Aunt Hazel, Delores, and Chunzila, who were riding in the old Ford pickup, down to the camp. We ate, then sat around in the log ceremony house, where we were to sleep. Delores couldn't get her mind off what was going to happen when she had to tell her dad she had wrecked his car.

"I know he's just gonna kill me!" she said over and over, wringing her hands, "Oh, jeez, what am I gonna do!"

As devoted as she was to her father, having him die seemed a less terrible alternative to face than having to tell him about the car.

The sun was just beginning to illuminate the sand bluffs across the creek when I got up the next morning, threw hunks of wood into the stove, opened the drafts, and jumped into the sack again to wait for the cabin to warm up. By eight we had finished breakfast and were ready to haul out to the hospital. Delores kept thinking up excuses to delay our departure.

"Henry, take them milk cans out to the creek and fill 'em up so's we'll have water when we get back."

She'd turn to Chunzila and say, "Son, get some more wood. Stoke up the stove again."

At last her mother, Aunt Hazel, announced we were leaving whether she was ready or not. We all went out into the cold bright morning and got into our old Dodge. Delores continued to find things to do in the log house.

Aunt Hazel reached across me and vigorously honked the car's horn. Delores finally climbed in and started wringing her hands again.

At the hospital Aunt Hazel took in the shopping bag with Uncle Bill's pants, shirt, shoes, and sweater, asking me to take his big sheepskin coat. When we walked into the room, Uncle sat up quickly and swung his legs over the side of the bed.

"Get that nurse in here. Tell him to take these damn needles out of my arms!"

Everybody tried to calm him down, but he was not to be calmed. He ripped the EKG electrodes off his chest and threw them on the floor. A beeper alarm went off. He pulled the tape off one needle and jerked it out of his arm. Blood started spurting all over the bed. He began working on the other arm and had it almost loose when the orderly ran in, hollering, "Grandfather, don't do that! I'll do it for you."

Being a Sun Dancer and having great respect for Eagle Feather was the orderly's undoing. He was just too slow and reluctant to touch the old man's body. Uncle Bill beat him to it, jerking the second needle free, blood squirting everywhere.

"Gimme my pants! Let's get outta here!"

The Uncle who had been near death three days before was nowhere in evidence. A couple of nurses came in and succeeded in pacifying him enough to get Band-Aids taped onto his arms.

All this time, Delores was out in the hall wringing her hands, biting her lips, and rehearsing what she was going to tell her father.

When I finished pulling on his boots and buttoning his coat, Uncle Bill asked where she was. Before I could answer he started hollering, "Dee-lores!"

Delores walked in the room looking pale and nervous, pulling at a button on her coat.

She began, "Daddy, the car . . ." He never heard her. Speaking out over her wavery voice in his big bass, he thanked her for washing his clothes and taking such good care of him while he was so sick. She kept trying to project the speech she had made up, but only her lips moved; no sound came out. Uncle was talking about how glad he was to see his relatives from the East, all the time heading for the exit. We all just followed him, right out the front door of the hospital. The doctor and the orderly were still trying to convince him he was too sick to leave as he sailed out the door with all of us in tow.

Out in the parking lot, his head swiveled as he scanned the cars for his favorite blue Ford.

"Over here, Uncle!" I said, opening the doors of the old Dodge station wagon.

"Can we all fit in that thing?" Uncle Bill was dubious. Both his daughter and his grandson Chunzila were built along his lines, size extra large. The three crammed into the backseat, while Aunt Hazel, Paula, Cody, and I got into the front.

"I s'pose this will be OK to get us back to camp. You should've brought my car, Hazel."

Impatient with Delores for chickening out, Auntie jerked her head toward her daughter and said curtly, "Talk to her!"

Uncle swung his broad face around, looking at his daughter expectantly. Delores blurted out her story in a small voice: "DaddyIwrecked . . . yourcarit . . . slidonthe . . . ice . . . itwentright . . . overthebank . . . intothebig . . . oak . . . bytheriver . . . youknow? I'm sosorry-y!"

Her father stared at her for a second then asked her if she'd been hurt. She shook her head wordlessly. Uncle was silent for a moment. Then, determined that nothing was going to ruin this day, he sat back with a big smile.

"Well, we'll just head over to Winner to see my friend Al after breakfast back at the camp. He'll trust me for a new car for sure!"

Al was the used car man Uncle Bill dealt with. His rates and prices were normally sky high, but he helped out Indians.

After breakfast, our second, Delores went to work at the Senior Citizen's, and the rest of us headed out to get Uncle a new car. The day was a beauty—sunny, with a warm breeze promising spring. As we tooled along through the res, the old medicine man began to tell stories. Every creek, every hill and bluff had a story associated with it. Some of them were personal to him, some were the stuff of Sioux history and legend.

"See that draw over there? Well, now, that's where I got my first eagle! I was only thirteen. I rode my pony past here to get to school. In those days, not only did the priests make us cut our hair, they even made us go to school! What do you think of that, Cody?"

Cody, riding in front on his mom's lap, agreed that was a terrible injustice. At eight he had long hair, but he also had to go to school.

"How'd you get the eagle?" Cody wanted to hear the rest of the story.

"Well, I was riding along. I had my double-barrel twelve-gauge slung on my back. It was kind of a sawed-off double my grandpa had used when he rode shotgun on the stagecoach. I seen this eagle settin' on a branch—right over there he was, see that tree? And I let him have it. Course I had to make offerings and such, and I had to cache the bird and the gun before I got to school. I made a lot of dancers and relatives happy with those feathers.

"Now, see that butte just to the north? No, that's not the one—the next one. Well, we trapped a Crow hunting party up there a long time ago."

Uncle was referring to something that had happened before he was born.

"Well, we had those guys surrounded. No way for them to get away. But they did! Our warriors chased them to the river. The Crows jumped right in an' swam acrost. Now, we weren't known as bein' swimmers, so nobody wanted to brave that water to get those guys. Those Crow men just stood on the other bank jeerin'. Kind of like, 'Nyah-nyah-nyah! You guys are chicken!' And we had to stand there an' take it."

Riding east on 18, we dipped down into a dry wash. Uncle Bill perked up. "Hey! Look at all that dead wood there! We'll pick that up on the way back! We'll all have a good Sweat later."

We got to Winner and pulled into Al's lot. Al saw the old man getting out of the car and came out to greet him. Uncle Bill and Al went into the office. Two minutes later, Al stuck his head out the door and hollered into the service area, "Jimmy, bring the red one down front!"

Jimmy stared, then called, "The good one?"

"Yeah, the good one. For my friend Bill. Make sure it's clean."

Uncle Bill called out, "Henry, come in here and meet my friend Al!"

I walked into the office. Uncle showed me the inventory sheet describing the car.

"What do you think?"

Al was offering a '63 Ford with everything. Only the air conditioner didn't work. I looked out the window as Jimmy drove up in a good-looking bright red car. I saw Auntie staring, with an expectant smile on her face.

"Looks good, Uncle!" I said.

Al made out the papers, and Uncle signed them without even looking at the car. We all shook hands and walked out to see it. The '63 Ford was sharp, with only a little rust, black upholstery, and good tires. Uncle Bill climbed into the driver's seat, Aunt Hazel got in back, and Chunzila got in front. I was amazed at how fast everything had gone.

"C'mon! Let's get outta here!" Uncle shifted into drive and the red car moved off smartly. I ran back to the Dodge and we took off, lagging behind the Ford.

When we got to the branch where Uncle Bill had spotted the dead wood, we saw the red car pulled over, the trunk open, and Chunzila already at work. Cody and I climbed down the bank and started gathering snags and branches. Pretty soon the trunk of the red Ford was full. Uncle stuck his head out the window and hollered, "Get that big one over there!" We continued piling up the wood till it reached the extended lid of the trunk.

"OK, let's go!" He had the red car rolling as Chunzila jumped in. Uncle didn't like to waste time.

As we followed the red car with its huge pile of wood rocking back and forth with every dip in the road, I said to Paula, "There's no way in hell all that wood's gonna stay in that car!"

As if to illustrate my point, the woodpile leaned precariously over as Uncle took a curve at sixty.

"Oh, Hank, you just don't have enough faith!" my wife chided me.

"Yeah, Dad, nothing's falling off!" Cody chipped in.

Sure enough, even after the two miles of off-road driving into camp, not one stick dropped off the load.

Uncle Bill backed up the car to the Sweat Lodge area, and we began unloading. Soon Chunzila had a good fire going, and the rocks were getting hot. I helped by cleaning out the Lodge and getting a bucket of water from the creek. The Bull boys came over from Two Strike community housing, and one volunteered to be doorkeeper.

We had our Sweat Lodge ceremony of thanksgiving, praying and thanking the Great Mystery for Uncle's wonderful return to health. Once again the medicine man's big voice led us in the songs of thanks and praise.

After the Sweat, we all had something to eat. At the table, Uncle Bill said to Chunzila and me, "We're getting short of tobacco. You fellows go out and get us some *chan-sha-sha* [red willow] and we'll make tobacco tonight."

So after we ate, Chunzila and I took off up the creek to gather some red willow. There was a large stand of it which we'd cut from before, and we got a big bunch of nice fat branches, rosy red, fresh and unscarred. "Don't take the scabby ones!" Uncle had warned.

That evening we cleaned off the big government surplus dining table and dumped the willow in the middle. The sheet-metal woodstove was red-hot, the big one-room log house cozy and warm as we started preparing the branches, scraping off the outer bark. Even Cody helped, gathering the piles of outer bark and throwing them into the stove. Pretty soon the six of us working had a nice stack of skinned willow branches, the pale green of the inner bark contrasting beautifully with the rose-colored outer bark of the twigs yet undone.

When we had finished all the twigs, we cleaned off the table and started again, this time scraping off the inner bark. Uncle began reminiscing, telling story after story, some serious, some hilarious, of adventures and misdemeanors from the past.

Some stories were at my expense. He told everybody about the great laugh he and Rube Fire Thunder, another Sun Dancer and medicine man, had when I saw them cutting down a green sapling and asked what the tree was.

"What does it look like?" was Rube's response.

"Kinnikinik," I replied. (*Kinnikinik* is the Eastern way of saying red willow or red osier dogwood.) My answer had them rolling in the aisles.

"What the hell's so funny?" I wanted to know.

With tears of laughter rolling down their faces, they replied in unison, "It *is kinnikinik!*"

It was the first time I had ever seen a green *chan-sha-sha*. My ignorance had Bill and Rube in stitches. And, of course, making fun of me was one of Uncle Bill's ways of teaching me to lose my self-importance.

At last we finished the scraping and had a big pile of *chan-sha-sha* in the center of the table. Chunzila got up and stretched, his bones cracking. He looked at me and jerked his head toward the door. He got his Pipe bag, and we walked outside into the frosty night.

The moon was almost full, giving us plenty of light to see where we were going as we walked up a draw on the other side of the creek. We climbed to the top of the bluff and sat down, wordlessly admiring the ghostly moonlit landscape. The scrub oaks, pines, and cedars of the draws made little dark islands in the immense expanse of the plains that stretched out before us. Way off to the south we heard an owl calling. We both shivered.

Spontaneously, we looked at each other and shook hands as an expression of our bond of friendship. Chunzila pulled out his Pipe, fitted stem and bowl together, and began filling it ceremonially. We each offered a short prayer, then smoked. When we finished, Chunzila said the ritual *"Mitakuye oyasin,"* took the Pipe apart, and put it away.

When we got back to the log house, everyone was asleep. We talked in low voices for a while, then hit the sack.

A couple of days later when it was time for us to leave, Uncle Bill made up a *wotawe*—a small protective medicine bundle—and hung it on the rearview mirror of the Dodge wagon.

"Leave it there! Don't take it off unless you get another car." These were his parting words. It's still hanging from the mirror of my thirty-year-old Chevy truck.

We told everybody we would see them in a couple of months for the Sun Dance.

A few hours later and 150 miles east on Interstate 90, we were glad to have that *wotawe*. The powerful north wind was blowing again, and managing the car on the icy road was difficult, even at thirty-five miles an hour. A quarter-mile ahead of us was a Consolidated Freightways tractor hauling tandem trailers. The rear trailer was whipping to and fro across both lanes. Finally, the driver lost control completely, and the rig double-jackknifed into the ditch on the south side of the road. A South Dakota state policeman traveling west made a U-turn and went to the driver's assistance.

A few miles up the road we saw the evidence of an earlier wreck that was spectacular. A cab-over tractor trailer had gone off the road and jackknifed. The cab had been torn completely off the tractor and was lying on its side twenty feet from the rig.

There was almost no traffic on the road. I stayed in the passing lane so that when the wind hit us I had both the slow lane and the shoulder as a safety margin. I couldn't keep our station wagon in one lane. A powerful gust of wind would hit us, and the car would slew into the other lane. We got to a part of the highway that was elevated on high banks above the surrounding plains. I couldn't help thinking that if we went off the road here we would be killed.

I slowed to twenty miles per hour just as a gust hit us like a giant baseball bat. The car slid off the road onto the shoulder, still doing twenty, going right to the very edge of the drop-off. Paula screamed. I yelled for Cody to get on the floor in back. The front wheels caught a patch of dry shoulder, and the car swung back across the slow lane and into the passing lane. The road was solid ice, no control possible. I gave the accelerator a quick blip and the car straightened out momentarily. Wind blasted us again, and we headed back toward the shoulder and drop-off. There were no guard rails along this road, but a short length of rail happened to be placed exactly where it could catch us as we headed off the highway.

We slammed into the rail and caromed off it back into the passing lane, accompanied by the loud noises of sheet metal grinding against the front wheel. I stopped on the shoulder. The wind whistling past the car was the only noise as we checked one another out in stunned silence. No one was hurt. The tension had been so great that we now began to laugh emotionally. It was great to be alive.

"Dad, there's a big piece of metal sticking out the side of the car!" Cody shouted excitedly.

I couldn't get out the driver's door, the wind was so strong, so I climbed over Paula and out the downwind door. I grabbed the piece of bodywork sticking out the side and wrenched it free, throwing it down the bank.

"What the hell! We didn't need that anyhow!" I was still

laughing, feeling wonderful to be alive and uninjured. Cody helped me bend the sheet metal away from the wheel.

Driving extra carefully, we made it to a service station, where we found no serious damage to the running gear of the car. The service man cut away the damaged fender and quarter panel. We continued on, arriving back home safely.

A few years later, when Aunt Hazel called me to be pallbearer, the events of the time when my Uncle saw the spirit women digging turnips kept running through my mind on that long haul across the plains to his funeral. His voice still comes to me, the kind words of his teaching echoing across time.

Preamble Ramble

Will is inexplicable. It enables people to do the undoable. Uncle Bill used to say, "You think too much!"

Just do it, don't think about it. Your thoughts will convince you it's impossible, and so it will be. Impossible to go four days without water, impossible to bring the dead back to life, impossible to heal, to carry the weight.

Will isn't something to be cultivated intellectually. It's an act—of faith, of brute strength, restraint, love, or enduring. Or something else.

Think about it after, not during the act of will. Thoughts only weaken you at those times.

CHAPTER NINE

The Blessing: Sun Dancing Is Difficult

We had undergone four days of purification. We were ready to dance. It was the summer of 1980, my fifth Sun Dance. The morning of the appointed day, we the dancers were solemnly led into the Mystery Hoop by Uncle Bill, to begin our four days of dancing and fasting, just as the fiery South Dakota sun was rising over the entrance to the circle.

Although I was his oldest apprentice, Eagle Feather liked to humble me by making me Tail End Charlie of the men's procession. In a sense, it was an honor, since right behind me came the leader of the women, Aunt Hazel.

Uncle Bill's Sioux Nation Sun Dance ground was a sacred circle about 100 feet in diameter, like all dance grounds, surrounded by a pine-bough brush arbor under which people sit watching the dancers. The drum sits in the South with the singers surrounding it, drumming and singing in unison.

By the second evening all of us were really thirsty and a little shaky, sucking on pebbles or bits of sage in a vain attempt to keep our mouths from being completely dry. Sun Dancing is hard. Going four days and four nights without food or water, dancing for four days in the hot sun, staring at the sun—these are some aspects of the Sun Dance that make it such a sacred and difficult devotion.

This year it was especially hard. Everything went wrong. There was no money to buy food for the singers, helpers, and spectators. A dancer was killed in a car wreck two weeks before. It seemed we wouldn't ever get it going. But somehow it all came together, and we had made it through the second day.

This second evening, a big wind came out of the West, turning the atmosphere brownish orange with blowing dust and sand. The sun was setting, everything bright but gloomy at the same time, very mysterious. Lightning flashed constantly, in sheets all over the sky, with dozens of jagged writhing strokes everywhere. No rain fell.

Prayers had been made that no harm would come to the Sun Dance and Grandfather heard them, because although lightning was striking on both sides of the camp it stayed in the sky above the campgrounds and sacred area, looking awesome and scary. Everybody was jumpy, running for cover to tents, cars, or *tipis*.

A man named Hawk had brought his wife all the way from Canada for a spiritual healing. Uncle Bill was famous for his healing powers, not only among his own people, but among other tribes as well.

Hawk's wife was a beautiful young woman around thirty. They said she had been cursed, that someone had thrown a hex on her. Some bad medicine men were known to do this. She was in agony all the time, saying it felt like knives running her through and through.

During this dusty lightning storm, Uncle Bill took her, her husband, and a couple of singers into the *Initi* to work on her. He used the Sun Dancers' Sweat Lodge. Most of the dancers were already asleep in the *tipi*, played out from dancing all day since sunrise. But some of us were around to watch the fire, hand in the red-hot rocks, and help out with the door.

We were way out on the open prairie, the rolling earth a pale green-tan from drought, with patches of *pejihota,* or sage, and *zuzecatapejuta,* or rattlesnake bush, dotting the plain. The dancers' *tipi* was just west of the fire, the sacred arbor to the east, and the creek maybe a quarter-mile beyond that. The wind was on us full force.

"Ho mitakuye oyasin!" Uncle Bill shouted from inside the Sweat. We threw open the blankets that served as a door. Hot steam poured through the opening.

"She's passed out," Uncle said. "You guys help get her out of here!"

Another dancer and I gently eased her through the low opening. Someone brought a folding chair, and we sat her down. She slumped over, unconscious. Hawk crawled out of the Sweat and stood over his wife. He was a big man, dark skinned, with long black braids hanging down to his belly. I could see his love for his wife in the way he looked at her. Nervous and helpless, he touched her.

Knots of veined lightning never stopped their flashing overhead, filling the sky. Thunderclaps came continuously from the strikes on both sides of the camp. The wind screamed around us, blowing showers of sparks and smoke from the fire-place. The orangy light was getting darker.

"I don't think she's breathing," said Hawk, in a conversational tone.

"What?" said Eagle Feather.

"She's not breathing." Hawk spoke up over the noise of the wind.

"See if her heart's beating," said Uncle. Hanging onto the towel around his waist, the husband kneeled and put an ear to his wife's chest.

"No, she don't have a heartbeat," he said quietly. About a mile down the creek a big bolt struck a tree with a shattering roar.

Everybody stood looking at Mrs. Hawk. She and her husband were strangers from another tribe, another country. "Hawk" was all we knew about them. It was all so casual. My heart was hammering, the blood pounding in my chest and ears. "God Almighty," I thought. "They're all gonna just stand there and watch her die!"

I screamed, "Get outta my way!" and jumped on her, using my hands and breath in a healing way—something like CPR, but I only learned CPR years later. I wasn't a healer, but I had to do something! "Breath of Life, help me!" I prayed. *"Onci malaipo!"* ["Have mercy, help me!"] I worked on her frantically, praying nonstop. Around me the wind and thunder roared. I begged the lightning Powers to give her life.

Finally, her arm twitched. She stirred, beginning to breathe.

"Ho!" someone behind me said. "Look at the rainbow!"

It stood majestically, a big arc right over the Sun Dance circle.

I ran to my pickup to get my star quilt and spread it on the ground. The lightning was still making a lacy network above us in the orange gloom. Some of the boys helped me lay Hawk's wife out on the quilt. She was barely breathing and not moving at all. I prayed, "Please don't let her die on that quilt!" The star quilt was a special gift from Delores.

I began blowing on her again and moving her arms. As if in a slow-motion film, the woman began to move. She opened her eyes. Big dark eyes, long black hair, pale smooth skin. "She's just marvelous," I thought. Her soft full lips opened. She struggled to sit up, propping herself on an elbow. She wanted to say something. I leaned over, trying to catch what it was.

In a small voice she said, "I was gone away, but you didn't let me go."

Then, "Gimme a cigarette, please?"

I lit one and put it between her lips.

She lay there, staring at the rainbow and the lightning-filled sky, dazed, too weak to move, slowly coming back to life. I held the Camel for her. She puffed feebly.

The sun set, the sky darkened. The wind died out as the storm moved east, and gradually the stillness of a quiet evening came over the camp. Then Hawk lifted up his wife and, half carrying her, took her over to their camper. They disappeared inside.

I sat on my star quilt in a daze. The last few minutes had been like some fantastic dream—the weather, the death and return to life, the rainbow. Everything so casual and slow-motion, no one thinking the woman would die or seeming to care one way or another, not a word spoken afterward. Not even a hint of thanks.

Hawk's camper began to move and slowly pulled out of camp. He and his wife were going back to Canada before the Sun Dance ended. They would never receive the blessing and healing bestowed by the sacrifice of the dancers.

After a while a powerfully built man walked over to me. He was about fifty, a full-blood Lakota. He wore a black Stetson and worn cowboy boots. The snap buttons on his Western-style shirt strained to keep the shirt closed over his barrel chest. I hadn't seen him at the dance before, but when he introduced himself I recognized him. He was a well-known medicine man from another reservation. I had heard a few medicine men worrying about how the heartbreaking death of his oldest child had affected his health.

"I seen what you done there," he said. "You done good, bringing her back like that. Really good! A lot of people couldn't do half as good."

He looked at me admiringly. He raised up his big hands in a gesture of prayer and praise. Still dazed, I couldn't think of anything to say.

"He made a mistake," he said, referring to Hawk. "But you done good. You had the faith and the hope, and it was strong enough to bring her back."

He looked at the wisps of steam still drifting from the Sweat Lodge.

"In that Sweat Lodge, in their efforts to heal her, maybe they got this high." He indicated a couple of inches with two fingers. "But out there," he pointed with his thumb to the Sun Dance arbor, "they could have reached the stars. She would've left here a healthy woman if he'd've brought her into that circle tomorrow for healing. The Sun Dance Power is that strong."

I looked at him, understanding what he meant. I had seen it happen before. Alcoholism, cancer, broken hearts, and broken families had all been mended by the sacred healing generated in the Sun Dance.

The wind had died, and the storm was east of us now, flashing and rumbling miles away. Overhead the stars were coming out. It had become a calm and beautiful evening. I looked at the man before me. In the darkness, his lion's face seemed to be glowing.

He said, "I seen how it's been this time, how difficult. Not enough food or help or nothin'! But that's the difference between you and him," he continued, still referring to Hawk. "If you had given up, none of this would've happened. But you had the faith and the hope, and you persisted. So, the Sun Dance is on, and the Power has hit, and we all can be blessed by it."

The fatigue of the long day descended on me suddenly, and my head fell forward on my chest. I jerked myself upright and looked at him. He arose from his squatting position with one easy movement.

"I'll leave you be," he said. "But tomorrow, will you do something for me? Sometime during the day, while you're dancing, if you see me sitting in the arbor watching the ceremony, let me know you recognize me. Just a nod or a finger movement is all I want. Good night."

"Now, why does he want that?" I wondered. Then I got it. Because I'd persisted, I'd had faith and hope, this holy man wanted a sign from me! The reality crashed down on my consciousness. "My God! He wants me to heal him!" I lay back on the star quilt, closed my eyes, and was instantly asleep.

Years later, my art department chairman sent all art faculty a form asking that we state the most outstanding accomplishment of our careers. I put down that I had brought a dead woman back to life at the 1980 Sun Dance. When he saw it, he laughed. I don't blame him. I couldn't expect him to understand that that achievement was much more important than any honor, Whitney show, or painting in a museum collection, of which I'd had many.

The next thing I knew, the *Eyapaha* [announcer] was announcing the dawn of the third day of the Sun Dance, and the light of *Anpao Wic'ah'pi*—Star of Understanding, the beautiful Morning Star—was streaming down on the camp from the still dark sky.

That afternoon, dancing as we faced West staring into the sun, one of the dancers passed out. She fell straight forward on her face. Eagle Feather came over and checked that she was okay, warning us not to touch her.

"Her vision's liable to come right now while she's lying there, so don't nobody bother her!"

There were twelve of us left. Our lips were coated with

dried white crud, and we had no more saliva left to lick it off. The woman who fell had been the only female dancer left. Four women and six men had walked out that noon, the third day the temperature had gone above 100. The remaining men were still standing, dancing, enduring, blowing our eagle bone whistles in time with the singers.

It was hardest while we were facing South and could watch the singers drinking soda and iced tea to keep their voices going. Once, that afternoon, as we faced the singers, my mouth was so dry I felt like I was going to vomit. But I didn't; I willed myself not to.

I was about ready to pass out when I noticed an old grandma, Mrs. Thin Elk, who was over eighty. She was sitting in the shade like everybody else, watching the ceremony. But unlike everyone else, who had a folding chair or blanket to sit on, Mrs. Thin Elk sat on the bare ground. She had no drink of any kind. Her big dark eyes, set deep in a wrinkled face, stared intently at the dancers. Her humility and endurance made me forget my own suffering.

I began to dance even harder. I was crying for her and the hardship she and all the elders had undergone. Then I saw the medicine man from the night before sitting behind her.

He was staring at me, tears running down his cheeks. I knew my own crying was making him cry. I made my whistle scream like the eagle and raised my hands toward him, this time giving the blessing instead of asking for one, as I might have in the past. His head dropped forward. He covered his face with his hands. I could see his shoulders shaking from the sobbing.

"Wakantanka onci." ["Great Spirit pity me,"] the drum sang, ["that my people may live"]. The song said it all. We the dancers suffered so that the people would live.

He wiped his eyes, looked up at me and smiled. He felt better already.

Future Times Ramble

There are people who can see into the future and make prophecies. Uncle Bill was one of those.

There have been many throughout history. The Tibetan Padmasambhava was one. In the eighth century he said that when iron birds fly and horses run on rails, the dharma, or teaching, would go to the land of the red man.

It's here.

CHAPTER TEN

Uncle's Prophecy: The First Healing

About the time Eagle Feather finished teaching me the medicine, he made a few predictions concerning my future. It was a beautiful bright November morning in '79, and we were sitting out back of my farmhouse by the Sweat Lodge, having a smoke. The leaves on the big box elder were yellow over our heads, and there were two yellowhammers, or yellow-shafted flickers, sitting in the tree making comments on our conversation. Occasionally, they would zoom down close to our heads and perch in another smaller box elder just to the north of the fireplace, watching us to see if we appreciated their acrobatics.

"Them birds sure like you, and they like this place. You know that, don't you, Nephew?"

I said I did, and that I was glad they were here.

"You're doin' good here, and you've got some good helpers 'round here. It's good to see that. But what I got to say now is somethin' about future time, so pay attention!"

Uncle Bill then began to lay out four things that he said

would come to me, events that he said would take place in the next ten years. These were actual prophecies.

At the time there was no way for me to know that this would be one of the last times I would be sitting with him as his student or apprentice. Within a year he himself would be making grass, as they say, buried on his hilltop Tipi Wakan, the grave guarded by *Wanbli Gleska,* or Spotted Eagle, the big bird sitting on a stone by his head and flying away only when someone approached to make prayers or offerings.

But on this sunny fall day, Uncle seemed to be vibrant with good health, full of stories that were lessons in themselves. When he started to predict, he got serious.

His first prediction concerned my daughter, Robby. She had graduated high school in 1976 and disappeared in the wilds of Washington, D.C. I hadn't heard from her at all in a couple of years. I had told Uncle Bill I was really worried that she had gotten in with rough company and was doing drugs, or worse.

Uncle now said matter-of-factly, "There's nothing you can do. She'll be back here in ten years. But she has to hit bottom before that happens." And that's pretty much how it happened. Robby did come back.

The next two prophecies concerned the spiritual and ceremonial life I would be involved in, statements that I thought were so far out as to be impossible.

"You're gonna have a Sun Dance here," he stated in a matter-of-fact tone. "It's gonna either be there," and he indicated a clearing a hundred yards away, "or down in that front field. It's up to you to figure it out."

I protested. It was impossible. I couldn't do it. We didn't have the singers and on and on. He roughly brushed my objections aside.

"That's your problem, not mine. I'm tellin' you, it's gonna happen."

He then prophesied that there would be a ceremony house standing near the Sweat in a few years. Three years later those prophecies were coming true.

The last prophecy made me very nervous.

"Nephew, I want you to be ready for this. A woman is coming here. She's got cancer. You're gonna cure her and she's gonna give you a lot of money. She'll be comin' in about three years and you must be prepared to go all out to help her!"

His statement shocked and upset me. I protested, saying that the plants had told me I would be curing other things. The year before, he had prescribed a strict way of praying to the plants in order to learn the nature of the healing I would be doing. The answers I got from the plants hadn't included healing cancer, or so I thought. Uncle Bill himself had helped me interpret the vision and the words I had received at that time.

"You told me that yourself, that I wouldn't be working with degenerative diseases!"

He fixed me with a piercing look. "Maybe you didn't understand as much as I thought you did. It was that, plus this too!"

He rolled his eyes skyward and muttered to himself something about slow learners.

"Dammit, Nephew, I'm tellin' you it's gonna happen, and I want you to be ready! So don't get caught asleep at the switch!"

I was full of questions. Nervously, I begged him to tell me how I should do it, what I should use, how I should go about it. He brushed me off, saying that if I was properly prepared I would know just what to do.

"I'm not doin' it, you're doin' it! And it has to be done your way. Don't be such a baby! You knew what you were gettin' into when we first started this!"

The yellowhammers started jabbering, *"Weet-weet-weet! Cha-cha-cha!"* as if to emphasize Uncle's point. They flew away into the woods. Case closed.

In the years after Eagle Feather's death, among several

other non-Indian healers, I met Jane, who was reputed to have cured lupus and other serious diseases. She was a big healthy woman, strong-willed and cheerful. I met some of the people she had helped, and they all treated her with great respect.

One day, Jane telephoned me. She wanted to come and see me later. That afternoon, after greeting me, she asked if we could go out to the Sweat Lodge and talk there. We were in the middle of a January thaw, no snow on the ground, and the weather was almost springlike.

We walked out back and sat down on the old Volkswagen bench seat that someone had donated.

"I just got some bad news," she began. "I went for a checkup. They told me I have cancer."

I sucked in my breath through my teeth. Jane reached in her pocketbook, pulled out a package of tobacco, and handed it to me. Later, I found out that she had a Cayuga grandmother, which is how she knew about the ceremonial gift of tobacco that one makes when asking for something.

I didn't know how to heal cancer—didn't know the first thing about it. I knew she was going to ask for a healing, and I was scared to death. I still didn't think I was supposed to work on things like cancer.

"I want you to help me. Will you? Please?"

I stared at the tobacco in my hand, my mind racing through possible excuses like, "Sorry, but I'll be outta town." Before I could think of a way out, Prince Albert on the wrapper changed into Uncle Bill for a split-second, and I remembered his prophecy.

I answered, "Yes, I'll do everything I can!"

Jane had cancer of the thyroid. The gland was getting bigger. She wanted to wait till her next medical examination in three weeks before she had the ceremony. That would put us in the middle of February. We sat there in the peacefulness surrounding the little Lodge, bathed in the weak but warm

January sunlight, and talked about what had to be done—preparing the food, gathering gifts for the helpers, and the rest.

It started getting colder, and Jane rose to leave. "I'll call you and let you know how I'm doing."

"Thanks," I said, "and remember to pray and keep your thoughts strong."

She said she would. I walked her out to her car.

Following the January thaw, we had a series of snowstorms, followed by a freak storm of freezing rain the night before we were supposed to make the first of Jane's four Sweat Lodge healing ceremonies. The first was supposed to be finished before noon, the second before sunset the same day, followed by the third and fourth the next day. But when my helper, Siniti, and I went out of the house before sunrise to start building the Sweat Lodge fire, we both slipped and fell down.

There was an inch of glaze ice on top of the foot and a half of snow already on the ground. The ice was so thick, it actually held our weight. We could walk on top of it. Then suddenly, it would give way, and we would break through, barking our shins on the thick crust of ice.

We had a terrible time of it, getting ready for the ceremony. All the snow and ice had to be removed from the Sweat, the fireplace, and the surrounding area. Then—something neither of us had foreseen—Siniti and I spent a long time looking for the rocks and wood, breaking the ice crust and groping around in the thick snow.

It took us four hours to get the fire going and the rocks hot. Despite the noon deadline for the first ceremony, it was eleven-thirty before we were ready to go into the Sweat Lodge.

During the weeks that followed Jane's request, I had prayed and concentrated, asking over and over for understanding as to how I could help her. The answer had come a week before, unexpectedly, as answers usually do. I was to make four bundles of medicine to use on her during the cere-mony. My confidence came back. I was relieved. I continued my prayer for guidance during this first Sweat,

In the steaming blackness as I was working on her, Jane said, "Oh! It's moving! I can feel it moving!" She felt the lump vibrate as I laid the medicine on her throat. I was praying hard for help and health.

When the first Sweat was over, I told Jane to go in the house and get some sleep before the afternoon ceremony. Then Siniti and I built up the fire again to heat up another set of rocks.

In an hour and a half, I took Jane back into the Lodge, and the doorkeeper handed in a good set of red-hot rocks. Jane was excited.

"It feels smaller! It's not as big as this morning!"

I was convinced that the disease was a goner already, but I didn't say anything, just sang my songs and continued to doc-tor her. The spirits were talking out in the center, and it was really hot.

We finished. When we came out, shaking hands with the doorkeeper, the steam pouring off our heated bodies, we were filled with energy. By rights, my helper and I should have been falling down with exhaustion after all the morning's work— breaking through the ice, shoveling snow, splitting wood, wrenching the rocks from the icy grip of the ground. Instead, we were all charged up.

Everyone was happy as we sat around the table eating the good food Jane had brought. We went to bed early, but Siniti said he would keep the fire going all night and have the rocks ready for us early in the morning.

We got up just before sunrise. It was a frosty clear blue morning. Out the window, I could see the smoke from the Sweat Lodge fire and knew that my helper was on the job. Paula said she would get Cody off to school and have breakfast ready for us when we came back to the house. Jane and I walked out into the crisp twenty-degree day just as the sun broke over the horizon.

Siniti greeted us with a broad grin. He was looking a little ragged from lack of sleep. He said the rocks were just about ready. Jane was prepared for the Sweat, clothed only in an old house dress, with an overcoat draped on her shoulders. She huddled close to the fire while I went behind the Sweat to take off my clothes.

Clad only in a towel wrapped around my waist, I went through the preliminaries quickly. After rubbing smoke from burning sage on ourselves, we crawled into the Lodge.

"Bring in those hot rocks!" I hollered at Siniti.

When the center of the little Lodge was filled with red-hot stones, Siniti handed in the bucket of cold water. I grabbed it and touched it to the stones.

"Welcome to our ceremony, Water of Life and Health!" I said. The helper covered up the door so that only the glow of the stones was visible.

I prayed, "Pity me, Grandfather, I'm doing this because I want to live in health with my relations!"

I poured on the water, and the searing, purifying, life-giving steam filled the little space. I began my first song.

Afterward, as we shook hands with Siniti and each other, I told Jane she didn't have anything to worry about anymore.

"All that's left is the thanksgiving, your last Sweat later this afternoon. Let's go eat."

We went into the house and had a healthy breakfast of scratch-built biscuits and gravy, eggs, and hot coffee.

We finished the thanksgiving around four that afternoon. Jane's friend Ann had come to cook the big meal that would finish everything off. She made a big roast of lamb with all the trimmings. The kitchen was hot and steamy. It felt and smelled so good when we came in out of the cold February dusk. The food was all laid out on the big round wooden kitchen table. I made up an offering for the spirits. Siniti ran it out to the Sweat Lodge and came back looking scared. He never did like to go out there after dark.

We sat at the table, eating to our hearts' content. Everything was perfect. It had gone so well; it had been difficult, but really good. Siniti and I had worked hard, and we had accomplished what we'd set out to do, to help Jane. All of us had the feelings of joy and elation that come at those times.

After dinner, Jane brought in a big bag and started giving presents to everyone. She made a lovely Giveaway.

The following week Jane called me up. She was on her way to the hospital, she said. Even though the lump was almost gone she was still scared and was planning to go through with the operation already scheduled for the next day. I told her that it was important for her to do what she thought was right, but I kidded her a little about being chicken.

"That thing is long gone!" I said. She said she would call from the hospital as soon as she could.

A couple of days later she let me know that I had been right. The doctors had gone in and found nothing malignant. She repeated the technical terms the doctors had told her. They didn't make sense to me, naturally, but I was happy that her mind was relieved.

During this time, we had been working hard building the log ceremony house. The house was patterned on Uncle Bill's ceremony house, but smaller. We had gone into the woods, cut down the biggest, straightest poplars, and logged out the eighteen-foot logs. We had everything finished but the roof. No one knew how to frame rafters, so I had decided we were going to have to hire a carpenter to do the job. But we had no money to buy the flat lumber, shingles, and whatnot, no money to pay the carpenter. So the job was stalled.

About a month after Jane's last phone call from the hospital I woke up early hearing the sound of a car pulling into the yard. I tugged on my jeans and walked outside to see who it was. Jane's friend Ann was sitting in her little car, the engine running. I tried to get her to have a cup of coffee, but she said she was late for work.

Ann stuck an envelope out the car window and said, "Jane's fine. She sends her regards, and she asked me to give you this."

I asked her what it was all about.

"I don't know," she said. "But it must be important 'cause she got me to come all the way out here to give it to you! I gotta be goin'. See you later!"

The sun hadn't yet melted the frost off the ground. I was shivering in my T-shirt as I went back into the house. What kind of message could Jane be sending me that couldn't wait till she visited again? I made coffee, poured myself a cup, sat down, and tore open the envelope. Fifty-dollar bills spilled into my lap—a lot of them. There was also a little piece of paper that said one word: "Thanks."

So the log house got finished. Jane's gift was just enough to cover the materials and labor. In a strange way, it helped fulfill two of the prophecies Uncle Bill had made, because he had also said, on that warm October morning the year before he died, that we would soon have a little ceremony house to sing in, and that it would stand somewhere nearby. We had our first sing in the log house four years after he died, under the roof Jane's gift made possible.

Unexpected Amble

I thought I had gotten used to Bill Eagle Feather's unpredictability and unexpected areas of knowledge. Listening to him lecture to university students gave me a whole new perspective on his dictum "Learn to keep your mouth shut!"

CHAPTER ELEVEN
Medicine and Art

One day I was sitting in my office in the art department of the University of Maryland when I got a call from a professor in American Studies. Would Chief Eagle Feather be willing to speak on Native American traditions concerning mental health? I said I would talk to him about it. It was the fall of 1978. Earlier that spring he had risen Lazarus-like from the Rosebud Indian Health Service hospital bed after seeing the ghost women digging *tinpsila*. Now he was back in Maryland visiting us.

A few times when Uncle came to Maryland to teach me or put me through a ceremony, I would get him speaking engagements at the local schools and universities. The honoraria from these engagements were a big help to his family. So, naturally, Uncle said he would be happy to talk about mental health. The arrangements were made. I was to make the introduction.

A couple of days later, we walked into an amphitheater filled with students and faculty. I gave a brief introduction: "William Eagle Feather, Sun Dance chief and medicine man of the Rosebud Sioux, will speak to you on traditional views of mental health." Then I took my seat in the front row.

I was by now used to Uncle's discursive 'round-Robin-Hood's-barn way of approaching a subject. This time, however, he seemed to be really stretching the limits of storytelling. He went on and on about how he had been asked to say the opening prayer and dedication of the new Indian center near Seattle, Washington, and how he had been warned by the local medicine men not to let a young man named Joe hold the Sacred Pipe during the ceremony.

Restlessly, I began furtively tapping my head—mental! mental!—as a sign to him to get on the subject. He paid me no mind but went on with his narration, which led to a talk about how we were relatives to all of creation. Even the worms were our relatives. I leaned forward in my chair and whispered, "MENTAL HEALTH!"

He fixed me like a bug on a pin with his piercing stare and said so everyone could hear, "Nephew, I *am* talkin' about mental health!"

Once again, he had embarrassed me—or, more precisely, I had embarrassed myself—in front of a crowd.

The gist of the story came out eventually. The young man he had been warned about had been acting very strange and was considered insane by the Indian population around the center. Uncle Bill related how he had taken Joe to his room and given him some medicine. He told Joe what to expect: in a little while he would use the toilet, but he was not to flush what came out of him. When Joe came out of the bathroom, Uncle Bill went in and fished a three-foot tapeworm out of the bowl.

"And that worm shares the red power with us humans! I cut him up and red blood came out!"

I still didn't get it, but Eagle Feather went on. "Here that worm was inside him, movin' around, his wigglin' affectin'

Joe's brain so's he couldn't think straight!" The worm's motion, according to Uncle, was causing Joe to hear things, including bells ringing.

"Next day we had a big cer'mony at the Indian Center. I made a good prayer and filled the Pipe. An' here when I handed the Pipe to Joe to hold, there's a big gasp from the people. They didn't know he was OK, back to normal because I got that relative—that worm—out of him. And, last I heard, he's still doin' fine."

Uncle Bill stated that some crazy people, like Joe, were just acting that way because of simple influences. Others were much more difficult to help and needed at least four singing ceremonies. And there were some who acted crazy because it was their nature, or because the spirits wanted them to be like that. Uncle said that he had talked some to psychologists about it.

How did he know these things? Mainly because he had been chosen by the spirits. He had spent a lot of time on a lonely hilltop, going without food or water for days at a time, praying for help, for communication, for the power to be of use to people, and the spirits had given him that power.

When he was finished, the audience asked many questions. Some he answered, to others he responded with his great line, "God gave you a brain, you figure it out." Or he said, "You already know the answer to that, but you forgot." As rude or blunt as his answers sounded, I knew from personal experience they were the truth.

During that same visit, I asked Uncle Bill to come with me to one of my university painting classes to talk to the students about *Lakol Wic'ohan*, the Indian tradition or way of life. In the past, Turkey had come to my drawing classes and posed with his old war bonnet for charcoal and watercolor sessions, but somehow I couldn't ask Uncle to do that.

It was toward the end of the semester, and the students had arranged their paintings on easels in a large semicircle for a final critique. It was an advanced painting class, and some of the work was very good.

After I introduced him, saying that Chief Eagle Feather would talk about Native American traditions, there was a very long silence. Uncle Bill was carefully looking over each painting without a word. I felt like nudging him, but after the American Studies affair I restrained myself.

Finally, in a measured, reflective way, he said, "Now . . . here . . . Who did this one?" A student raised her hand. "Well. Whatcher name?" "Gina." "Well, Gina, there's a lotta spirits in this pitcher, just look there. You painted a pitcher of yourself but right there, back of your head, I'll bet you didn't even know you made a pitcher of your guardian spirit. Did you?"

Gina's mouth dropped open. She hadn't known, but now she and everybody in the room could see the image emerging from expressionist swirls of paint.

Uncle Bill began critiquing every painting. My feeling of impatience changed to amazement. As far as I knew, he didn't know a thing about art, yet from pure intuition and sensibility he was not only speaking of subject matter, as he did for Gina's painting, but also saying things that I might have said concerning composition, form, and color.

"OK, Dan. Now. Take your pitcher an' turn it upside down." I was dumbfounded. Having students do this is standard practice in any critique. He went on to suggest to Dan that there would be a better balance if he added some color or texture to some part of the painting. Then, he explained, the spiritual value as well as the composition would be enhanced. Dammit! He was right!

"Now, Katherine. Here. Look at all this reeeally nice stuff you put out at the edges of your pitcher. Why, that's even better than what you put in the middle!"

"Good night!" I thought to myself. "He's hit on a criticism that's a hundred years old." Since the Impressionists, critics have remarked that the edges of a painting are often better than the main part. One of my teachers at Columbia, Meyer Schapiro, a famous art historian and critic, suggested that it was because artists felt they could be more adventurous in less important parts of the painting.

Uncle Bill talked about the paintings for an hour. He left me very little to say. The students were no less amazed and in awe of the old man's wisdom than I. They actually gave him a hand when the session was over.

On the way home I asked him if he had ever looked at paintings before. "No, that's the first time. But I got eyes, an' it was all there in those bee-you-tiful pitchers, now, wasn't it?" I had to admit that it was!

Faith Ramble

The line between ignorance and faith is thin and fuzzy. Do we do things—perform acts—out of faith or plain ignorance, being too dumb to know not to do them?

The song says, "Look to the West. Your Grandfather is sitting there, looking this way. Pray to him. . . ."

Standing up on the hilltop, fasting and thirsting, trying to pray. Looking West, in my ignorance, I don't see anything but earth and sky. But Uncle said so, so I keep on praying.

Even if you don't have faith, acting like you do helps.

CHAPTER TWELVE

Uncle's Teaching: Fear Defeats My Final Lesson

Bill Eagle Feather was truly impressive in his hundred-eagle-feather chief's bonnet, but he used his regalia only for special ceremonies. The greatest part of the time he wore old Levi's, worn cowboy boots, and a chambray cowboy shirt that stretched tightly over his big belly.

Although there were always plenty of men around his camp on the Rosebud Reservation to help him with the daily work of cleaning up, butchering meat for the family, repairing the old trucks and cars, and cutting wood, he was never shy about pitching in and doing the most menial chores. It never ceased to astonish me that this elder holy man thought nothing of crawling under a vehicle and repairing or replacing its parts. He was a great believer in setting the humble example. Being of service was his life's work. So he was not only a medicine man—a priest and healer—but he was also, by example and otherwise, a great teacher.

Uncle Bill had the darndest way of teaching. Sometimes he

would set things up so he had my undivided attention in some quiet place. But lots of times he would start laying something out when I was really busy or preoccupied with something else, or when I was driving the old rattly Ford pickup that made so much noise I could hardly hear him speak. Educators would call his way of teaching experiential, in that it was almost always accomplished through doing, not talking. If you wanted to learn, you had to work. Most of the medicine men teach this way.

He would say, "You 'n' me are gonna get wood for the ceremony fire. Get that Ford cranked up!" He would head for the shed next to the log house to get the chain saw and ax, shouting over his shoulder, "If you hafta jump-start it we'll take your pickup. I don't wanna walk home out of those draws."

We would go bouncing over the plains, scaring the dickens out of the cows and prairie dogs with the tinny jangle of the old Ford's rusty body and its blown-out muffler. Amidst the banging, jangling roar he would sing a ceremonial song, quietly, and finish by saying what the song was used for. He would ask, "You got that?"

I would sing back to him the 40 or 50 percent I had heard. His lips would tighten with impatience. He would sing it again, exaggeratedly slowly, and repeat, "You got it?" If I didn't have it, he would start muttering about slow learners, his big head swiveling back and forth, gray braids swinging, as he scanned the countryside for dead wood.

"There! That's a dead ellum"—his way of saying *elm*— "down there in that draw! Cut back th' other way. Watch that drop-off! Can you make it down there?"

I would shift into first and ease the truck over the rim and down what appeared to be a 50 percent grade, sliding in the sandy soil. If Uncle wanted us to go down there, I had faith that there was a way out of there, even with a full load of wood. It was one of the things I learned from him—to have faith.

Whatever it was that Bill Eagle Feather saw in me, I always had the feeling he saw more than I wanted him to see. Like any neophyte, as soon as I began to get some understanding, I thought I knew it all. The old saw "A little knowledge is a dangerous thing" certainly pertained to me in my elementary state of education, and he saw that clearly.

This was why part of his teaching included making it a point to ridicule and even humiliate me in the presence of others. Humbleness was a great virtue in his way of doing things and, boy, did he humble me, over and over. My inflated sense of self-importance took a serious beating in his wise and capable hands. The medicine was for doing the Great Spirit's work, for helping people, for promoting life and health. Arrogance had no place in it. That was his philosophy.

One day, I saw a man who had requested a ceremony for his sick wife shove some money in Uncle Bill's pocket. Uncle read my mind and later said to me, "Narcise is a poor man. He prob'ly gave me every dollar he had to treat his wife. I seen your eyes. You're like ever'body else, thinkin' a medicine man's makin' lots of money, an' that maybe you will too. Don't ever get in the way of doin' it for the money. Most folks are too poor or don't have the understandin' they need in order to know that they gotta give for what they get. Don't ever get in the way of countin'! Don't count, just do your best and help people. If you start countin', it'll really screw you up!"

In spite of his advice, I did count for a while. My wife reminded me of Uncle's kind words before I got too screwed up, and I stopped.

The basis of the medicine teaching that I received from Eagle Feather and other men and women who followed the traditional path might be summed up in the following words: *akihoka, waableza, tawacin,* and *kiciyuonihate;* this translates, roughly, to "skill," "sharply perceptive and active seeking," "mind" or "willpower," and "rendering respect." Only through following and actively living out these ideals can a person arrive at an enlightened state in which he or she is able to do some good for other people and the Creation as a whole.

So Uncle would say to me, *"Skuyayo, Tunkska, niakihoka!"* ["Remember always, Nephew, your skill!"] The point he was making was that whatever skills I had acquired in my life-time—whether in lovemaking, art, teaching, or healing—they should always be actively employed.

I asked him what that word *akihoka* meant. He replied, "Same as the white man's word *technology*." I didn't think that was the original meaning of the word, but I kept quiet. Years later, I found out that the word *technology* comes from the Greek *techne*, meaning "skill," so his translation was right on the mark!

He would say, *"Skuyayo, Tunkska, akita mani yo!"* ["Remember, Nephew, pay attention as you walk this life path!"] He was reminding me to use my *waableza,* my keenest powers of seek-ing and observation. For him it was a fact that 90 percent of the phenomenal world passed unseen to most people and that because of this they remained unenlightened.

He used to say, "This Earth is sacred! Don't you ever forget it! She's our Mother an' our Grandmother, all wrapped up in one. Always give her honor an' respect. She's all we got, an' she's given us everything—everything! The food, the medi-cine, our clothes, even our cars come out of her. She's treated us so-o kindly! Don't be one of them that pollutes and filthies her."

He liked to talk about *Mitakuye oyasin,* saying that we were relatives to the whole Creation—not only to the human beings, but to the animals, birds, and plants. Uncle Bill felt that the non-Indians had forgotten this, and that's why the world was in such sorry shape. The white man was never taught that the Earth was sacred, so he dumped on her and made the water undrinkable and the air unbreathable. He killed and made slaves because he never understood that we were all relations. Uncle believed it was ignorance and greed that made the white man have no respect for Creation.

Racism was all part of that, he said. "Because us Indians suffered so much at the hands of the *wasicun,* we started hating him as much as he hated us. We older ones have mostly got over that, but the young ones still have that hate in their hearts. You know about that, don'tcha?"

I said I did. I had seen it and experienced it.

Uncle continued. "Well, it took me a long time to get that hatred out of my heart. My understanding came through a vision of the blood." I asked him what he meant. "Well, for us Red men, the color red is sacred. Our skin is red, our blood is red, the sacred cedar wood is red—many sacred things are red. One day it come to me that if you cut a black man, his blood isn't black, it's red. Same for the white man and the yellow man. It was then I understood that this was the greatest gift from Above—the gift of life itself—an' we shared that gift with all the people on Earth, an' the animals too! It was then I truly understood the meaning of 'All my relations.' We can't hate those other colors, they are our brothers! That's why I preach so much about the colors, an' having respect, an' love for our relatives!"

A few years before he died, Eagle Feather spent the better part of a morning staring at me without saying a word. I was working around the camp. I had gathered all the knives and axes and was sharpening them on a piece from a big broken grindstone wheel. All the time I was doing this, he kept fixing me with that piercing look of his. It was obvious he was thinking about something. I was used to this, so it had ceased to bother me. He was always sizing me and the others up.

I took a break and went into the log house to get a cup of coffee. He came in behind me and poured himself a cup also. We went outside and sat down on the old car seat propped up against the trunk of the box elder tree. I pulled out a pack of cigarettes, and we both lit up.

"What's on your mind, Uncle?" I asked.

He kept looking at me silently. Taking a deep pull, he exhaled and said, "I could make a *Yuwipi* man out of you in a week!"

I looked away from him and mentally said, "Oh, no, I can't handle that!"

He kept on staring. "A week's all it'd take me!" he said softly.

A *Yuwipi*—"They tie him up"—is a very special kind of medicine man, one who actually puts his life on the line for the people he is trying to help or heal. The best *Yuwipis* can heal almost any disease through their act of devotion and sacrifice.

At this point I myself on occasion had tied Uncle up in these ceremonies. When I did, since I was skeptical of the process and thought there could be sleight of hand involved, I always tied him as tight as possible. The hands are tied behind the back, index finger to index finger, middle finger to middle finger, and so on to the pinkies. I pulled the knots tight. Then I put the blanket over his head, with a rawhide slipknot noose around his neck and seven knots tying him all down his back to his ankles. When thus laid down in the Altar he was incapable of movement. I could hear his labored breathing inside the blanket. A couple of times in those ceremonies we'd had to sing the Emergency song when the spirits didn't come right away. Uncle Bill, after all, had already had a couple of heart attacks. Once it was close; he almost stopped breathing.

I didn't want to be tied up like that. The prospect scared me silly. I didn't have the faith to do it. I looked at Uncle Bill. He was still looking right through me. This was something I couldn't say yes to, but I sure couldn't say no to my Uncle Bill.

"Take me 'bout a week," he repeated.

At that instant, there was a commotion up on the hill by the

Sun Dance arbor, and somebody started yelling incoherently. The screen door slammed on the log house as Aunt Hazel and Oray went flying out up the hill. Uncle Bill and I jumped up and joined them. A fight had broken out between three young men, and one boy had been slashed. The next hour was taken up with a run to the hospital.

Once again, Uncle Bill had read my mind. He never again brought up the subject. In the years since his death, I have, in my memories, returned over and over to that moment. If only he had waited for the following year! I would have welcomed it then—been honored by it then! In the year that followed, I learned how to have faith and everything else I would have needed—the skill, the will, the trust and confidence in the spirits—to become a good *Yuwipi.*

But it passed me by. It's true, sometimes you do get only one chance. You'd better be ready to grab it when it comes. That's what the Romans meant by *carpe diem*—seize the day! We may think we have a lot of time, Eagle Feather always reminded us, but in truth we have only a little time on this Earth.

Ramblin' Without Eyes and Ears

"Tunkasila *gave you eyes and ears. Are you gonna take the responsibility?" Uncle Bill meant that the gifts of sight and hearing carry with them the responsibility of using those faculties to the limit.*

After more than fifty years of teaching, I know that when students say, "I see," "I hear," "I understand," none of the above is happening. And I have proven it to class after class through giving them the simple task of making a line drawing of what is in front of them. In some of the drawing classes 100 percent of the students could not see, could not hear the instructions, or could not or understand them. This was equally true for full professors in the university honors program, as I proved to them once, to their disgust.

Me too. I can be as deaf and blind as the next one from time to time. But I'm trying to use my gifts and not sleepwalk through this precious life.

Sitting Bull's vision, which he got at the Sun Dance of June 21 or 22, 1876, was of soldiers falling into camp. The Spirit told him, "I give you these because they have no ears."

A few days later, on June 25, Custer and all his men fell because they had no ears.

As Uncle would say, "You got a brain, you figure it out."

CHAPTER THIRTEEN

Deaf Eddy:
The Second Healing

In late fall 1983, we were putting the finishing touches on the Eagle Voice log house on our farm in Maryland, getting ready for the first ceremony there. It would be for a woman whose diabetes was causing her to go blind. Her circulation was so bad, the doctors were talking about cutting off her leg. But through the mystery of the ceremony, her eyesight would be restored, as would the circulation to her legs. She would lead a normal life after that, driving her car cross-country and hiking, and finally dying a natural death years later.

Now, we were getting ready. The roof was finished. The sheet-metal cordwood stove, along with its stovepipe, was in working order, and we had a nice fire going to keep warm. We were mixing up mud and chinking the house. Some of the crew were working on the inside, and some, on the outside. Much of the chinking was done, but in places we still had a clear view of the outdoors between the logs.

The locusts, box elders, and chokecherries surrounding the

log house had long since dropped their leaves. A north wind was blowing. The hawk was flying, as they say. Winter was on its way.

Lyn came inside the log house, where I was working, and introduced me to a couple of friends she had brought, Joe and Ed. I asked Joe to help on the outside, and Ed stayed inside with me.

As Ed and I worked, I started talking to him about what we were doing and asking him if he had participated in any ceremonies before. He didn't look at me or answer. I tried again. He refused to speak.

"What is with this guy?" I thought to myself, and went outside to talk to his friend Joe. I told Joe that Ed seemed to me to have an attitude problem.

"Oh, it's not that at all!" he said. "Ed is stone deaf. He doesn't even realize you're talking to him unless he sees your lips move. He's a good lip reader, so make sure he's looking at you when you speak."

Mentally kicking myself for assuming something negative, I went back inside. I should have picked up on his deafness, since Ed talked in a monotone unusual in hearing people, but which I'd heard in deaf people before.

Outside, the rocks had been gathered and the fire lit for an evening Sweat Lodge ceremony. I asked Joe if Ed had come looking for help for his deafness. Joe said that he had.

We finished troweling and fingering the last load of mud in place. There was more to do, but it was time to quit and concentrate on the Sweat. The log house looked beautiful, almost finished.

It was the product of many loving hands and much effort. We had started it two years before. It had a red clay floor, no plumbing or electricity; it was as simple and primitive as Uncle Bill's ceremony house out on the reservation. It was sixteen feet square on the inside. We had cut all the logs, each eighteen feet long, and built it square, level, and true. Some of the butt logs weighed over six hundred pounds, and we had manhandled them out of the woods ourselves. All of us were proud of what we had accomplished.

As the sun neared the horizon, the beautiful November afternoon began to turn cold. A stiff breeze came up, and black clouds moved across the western sky. It was going to be a frosty night.

The people stood around the fire, watching the glowing rocks and embers. Everything was ready. We stripped, rubbed the smoke from a bunch of smoldering sage on ourselves, crawled into the Lodge, and waited in silence as the doorkeeper brought in the red-hot rocks. We were unified in our desire to help this newcomer Ed.

The following week, everyone showed up again, including Joe and Ed, and we finished chinking up the log house. While we were working, I asked Joe how everything was going.

"Fine," he said. "I really appreciated the ceremony last week." I asked him how Ed liked it. He said that Ed was still a little freaked out about what had happened.

"What do you mean?" I asked.

"Didn't he tell you? Ed heard every word you said in there. And when the door opened at the end, he was deaf again."

Ed was standing there. I touched his arm to get him to look at me. I asked him if this was true. He said it was. I told him that if he really wanted to hear again it would take more time. He said he would keep coming to the ceremonies.

Three weeks later, I came home from work really tired. I lay down on the couch to watch the news on TV. I was half-asleep when Cody called out that there was a phone call for me.

"Who is it?" I asked.

"Eddy."

"Eddy who?"

"You know, Eddy." There were a couple of Eddys who came around. I couldn't make the connection to Ed.

I hollered, "Choctaw Eddy from Oklahoma?"

Cody hollered back, "No, Deaf Eddy!"

What the dickens? Ed couldn't talk on the phone. He couldn't hear. He and Joe had developed an elaborate code for communicating by phone, but I didn't know it.

When I answered, a voice trembling with elation said, "It's me. I can hear. This is the first time I have used the phone normally in eight years! I woke up this morning and heard my neighbor's dog barking! I didn't know what it was. Oh God, Uncle Henry, thanks!"

A little over a year later, on a beautiful warm afternoon, Joe, Ed, and I sat down together under the big box elder. The air was filled with spring's promises; the grasses and leaves were just beginning to show their pretty green faces. I asked Ed to tell me his story.

He told me that his deafness was due to some childhood trauma or disease. About a week before he had first come out to the farm, he had once again visited the otolaryngologist. After examination and X rays, the doctor had told him there was "no visible sign of any structure." In other words his middle ears had completely calcified and become bony material. Ed was told that there was no possibility of his ever recovering his hearing.

As he told of his first visit, when we were doing the chinking, it seemed as though he hadn't come looking for or expecting any help. Rather, he had come out of curiosity, and because his friends were coming.

He said that once we had gone into the Sweat and the door had been shut, he was closed off from communication with me because it was dark and he couldn't see my lips. He was scared when a voice began to speak to him, telling him everything I said. When the door was opened at the end he was still deaf, and the voice was gone.

By the fourth ceremony he could hear me directly while the door was closed, but his deafness still resumed at the end of the Sweat. It was four days after that, the Thursday following the final ceremony, when the neighbor's dog awoke him in the morning, and he could hear normally.

Because of his deafness, he had been fired from his job the year before. It had been judged too dangerous for a deaf person. He now had his old job back.

"I've had a hard time accepting having my hearing back," Ed revealed. "Frankly, when I was deaf I got away with a lot of stuff, and people excused me because of my deafness. I'm not sure I want the responsibility of hearing again."

I told him that he'd better make up his mind fast to accept the responsibility, or the gift might be taken away by the spirits who had helped him.

Ed continued to come, helping out, cutting wood, cleaning up, and participating in the ceremonies and prayers. Later that year, in August, he came to me and in a voice trembling with emotion thanked me for the help he had received. He said that he had been "clean" for one year—he had stopped using drugs and booze. He felt that his life had been given back to him.

Eddy got a job in Pennsylvania and moved away. He still comes back from time to time.

"Don't Look Back,
Somethin' Might Be Gainin' on You!"

I think about old Satchel Paige's admonition often. Keep on going. Look up ahead. Somethin' might be waitin' for you, he might have said.

As I age the images of the past seem to get sharper, coming on me when I least expect, uncalled, the triumphs and blunders of younger days flashing equally in my mind, causing me to grin or squirm.

I'm grateful for all the chances I took. I'm grateful that my upbringing, what I got from my folks, let me take those chances, even the ones that weren't too bright—like flying an airplane inverted on VJ day, or spinning a Model A on a dirt road for the hell of it.

Those are two memories that still make me squirm. I could have killed myself and never been able to take the good chances that came to me in later life, never had the chance to follow Turkey's, or Uncle Bill's, or Grandpa Henry's teachings.

Today is a good day to die. Better be sure it's for something worthwhile.

CHAPTER FOURTEEN

Carrying on the Teaching: "Healing and Helping This Precious Life to Redeem"

In 1975 and 1976, Grandpa Henry Crow Dog instructed me as to how to build a Sweat Lodge and conduct the Sweat Lodge ceremony. Grandpa was the first one to tell Paula and me to take the teaching back home and use it for, in his words, "healing and helping this precious life to redeem." He was a man who lived by the words he had roughly lettered on a sign at his place, Crow Dog's Paradise, at Grass Mountain on the Little White River: "Kind Words Never Die," the sign read.

I first met Bill Eagle Feather on Crow Dog's Paradise. The first time I was pierced, in 1976, it was Uncle Bill who was conducting the Crow Dog Sun Dance while Leonard Crow Dog was in federal penitentiary for being the leader of the Wounded Knee protest. Uncle and Henry Crow Dog had a cordial relationship, but they weren't close.

Paula and I have vowed that Grandpa Crow Dog's kind words, and the words of Bill Eagle Feather and all our teachers, will continue to live.

Besides "God gave you a brain, you figure it out!" Uncle Bill had a number of expressions that he repeated over and again. He chastised me often with "When are you gonna learn to keep your mouth shut?" He didn't want me or the others he was teaching to talk about the medicine to others. He thought there were too many people acting like what John Donne called "blind mouths," bragging to aggrandize themselves, thus missing the essential subtle vibrations of wisdom and knowledge all around them. He was teaching us not to blab about what we know—not to play what I call "spiritual one-upmanship."

Early in our relationship, Bill Eagle Feather knocked me out during one of his teaching sessions by announcing that every human has to find the answer to four questions. He said them in Lakota first, which I had a hard time understanding, then English.

Who am I? How did I get here? What am I doing here? Where am I going from here?

He usually followed the final question with his piercing, meaningful glance, saying, "An' you *know* where. We have but one more journey to make!"

What blew me away was that these were the same four great questions the Western philosophers spoke of. Gauguin inscribed them on one of his major paintings. Uncle always said that the simplest questions were the hardest.

Bill Eagle Feather lived and acted simply and humbly. He was anything but simple. He was sharp as a tack. Like Turkey Tayac, he sometimes played the fool to elicit a response or to see how people would react. By turns, he occasionally played me, Oray, and a couple of other students for the fool. He was right. He had amused scorn for any hint of arrogance or presumptuousness, particularly in professionals—doctors, for instance. That is part of my inheritance from him.

For a period of four years after Uncle Bill's death, I was invited to speak to certain groups at the University of Maryland's School of Medicine in Baltimore. In 1984 I was speaking to what I thought was a group composed exclusively of medical students. I spoke of the power of Indian medicine and the humility of medicine men, who did not charge for their services. I told the students that they were the coming generation, and it was up to them to walk a path away from the profession's traditional arrogance. They could make medicine more human.

It was a large room. At the end of my talk, an imposing white-bearded man I had not seen approached me. I realized he was one of the professors.

"Listen, we're getting tired of you fellows coming in here telling these kids how arrogant we are!"

I said, "You mean, someone else has said the same thing?"

"Yes, the last guest speaker used the same line!"

Hesitantly, I replied, "Well, didn't it occur to you that there might be a grain of truth there somewhere?"

That was the last time I was invited to speak at the School of Medicine.

Around the same time, I went to see my doctor friend, a distinguished physician, head of a big department at University Hospital. He remarked on the Sun Dance scars on my chest and asked if that was part of the medicine I was studying.

I took the opportunity to ask him why modern medicine didn't pay more attention to some of the wisdom the old medicine men had concerning the healing of disease. I pointed out that after all the millions spent on cancer research, the medical establishment still didn't have the answer. My Uncle Bill, on the other hand, had cured cancer with a ceremony.

My friend drew himself up and huffily inquired why, if my

Uncle was so damn smart, he didn't publish his findings. He didn't read or write English, I told him—a slight bending of the truth.

Doctors' attitudes are changing; at least, the attitudes of some are changing. In 1993 I was invited to speak at a large conference by the National Institutes of Health's Office of Alternative Medicine. I participated on a panel with a distinguished physician, who served as director of research at a major pharmaceutical lab. I was dumbfounded to hear what this doctor had to say.

He related six case histories, all declared by the attending M.D.'s to be terminal, inoperable, or incurable. All six recovered their health and became active. The only common denominator in their healing was prayer.

When I was called on to speak after him, I began by saying that I never imagined I would hear a physician say such a thing. That got a big hand from the auditorium full of health professionals.

My own presentation was on healing plants, of which I had a bagful. I played show-and-tell with yellow dock, yarrow, and eight other medicinal plants.

Generally speaking, doctors know little or nothing about the medicinal value of plants and food. Even our most common foodstuffs—corn and oats, for instance—can be used medicinally.

I related the story of a man with hepatitis C whose liver was enlarged and precancerous. The doctors wanted to place him on a course of Interferon, which would make him sick as a dog, cost fifteen thousand dollars, and give him a 25 percent chance at complete remission. I suggested that eating dandelion daily might help. He followed my suggestion. A year later, his doctor told him his liver functions were "normal."

It is true that disease may be cured or helped with plants or with "medicine." It is equally true, as the director of research said, that disease can be cured by prayer, by pure will to live, and by concentration, intent, or sacrifice.

In 1985 I was Sun Dancing next to my *Hunka,* or brother, Dallas Leading Fighter. Early in the morning of the first day he told me that he was going to pierce and stay tied to the Tree all four days, a sacrifice of suffering and endurance. His wife, Mary, had cancer, and he was asking the Above to heal her through his sacrifice.

He did this for four years. On the last day of the fourth year, Mary came to the arbor to watch him break. She was free of cancer.

That is the meaning and value of sacrifice. All the ceremonies—Sun Dance, Sweat Lodge, Vision Quest, Pipe, *Lowanpi*—are done for one purpose only, and that is the promotion and redemption of life and health. Miraculous healings have been accomplished through ceremony and sacrifice.

The leader of the Sun Dance is sometimes called the intercessor. That's all a medicine man or woman is: a go-between. Medicine men and women do not brag about the diseases they have cured. If he is wise enough and humble enough, he knows that all he is, as my Uncle Bill said, is a custodian, a vessel to be used by the spirits. He is owned by the spirits. He is worn by the spirits, like a coat or a shield. He, or she, is a helper, that's all; a spiritual person, working for the people. A medicine man rarely calls himself by that term. The people may call him medicine man; he humbly calls himself a helper. The spirits heal; all he does is facilitate by helping.

One evening in the summer of 1993 we were having a *Lowanpi.* Lyn, I believe, had been to the Folklife Festival on the Mall in Washington, D.C., that day. There, she had met a Quechua Inca *brujo,* or shaman, from Peru and had invited him and his family to the ceremony. The shaman had been very excited at the prospect and said he would be there.

We had the ceremony, and at the end, when the food was

being served, in walked the shaman and his two sisters. They had gotten lost.

Both he and I were happy to meet each other. One of the sisters spoke English, and she translated. He sat on a cushion between Paula and me, with the sisters on either side of us. He liked the traditional food—the *wohanpi*, the *wojapi,* and the rest.

He told me the story of how his *brujo* had taught him. Toward the end of his training he was given a large drink, a tea made of psychotropic plants. Under the influence he realized for the first time in his life the tragic conditions of Indian life. He began crying his heart out, sobbing, "the poor Indians, the poor Indians," over and over. The *brujo* whacked him on the head and hollered at him, "Stop crying! Laugh!" Almost instantly he was overtaken with gut-busting laughter, uncontrollable. This was the breakthrough the *brujo* had been preparing him for!

About one-thirty in the morning, as people were leaving, I walked the shaman and his sisters out to their car. Through the English-speaking sister I learned that he was very interested in medicinal plants in North America. I told him that there were more than fifty medicinal plants growing on our farm and that he should come back tomorrow when I could show them to him. He was disappointed. He couldn't come because he was scheduled to give a talk at the Smithsonian.

"We medicine men," he told me, "have the responsibility to take care of these plants and, through them, to take care of the people."

"Hey," I said, "I'm no medicine man! I'm just the janitor 'round here, keeping the place clean."

When his sister translated what I had said, the *brujo* started laughing so hard he almost fell down. I was a little upset. "What the hell's he laughing at?" I wanted to know.

She smiled, "He says that's what he is, too!"

I said, "Well, if that's the case, maybe we ought to be calling each other Brother!"

She translated. He looked me in the eyes and said the Quechua word for *brother.* I only wish I could remember it.

At the car we shook hands, then embraced. I wanted him to come back, but he said he had to leave for Peru after the speech at the Smithsonian. He waved as they left. It was the last time I saw him. Wherever you are, Brother, I hope you are healthy and happy.

Influence Ramble

*Life is a sum of influences. Who am I? How did I get here?
What am I doing here? Where am I going from here? The
answers to Bill Eagle Feather's four questions all depend on
influence.*

CHAPTER FIFTEEN

"Tunkasila, Ta Wokunze Ca Lena Cicu"

In the words of the old ceremonial ending, or Quitting song, "Grandfathers, your influence is in all these gifts. . . ." My grandfathers, grandmother, mom, dad, great-aunts and uncles, all my blood relatives as well as my beloved wife, children, teachers, and friends have exercised a wonderful and sometimes mysterious influence on my life. I am grateful for them and for that influence. The memory of those who have gone endures to this day, as do their gifts.

We put C'uwi Wanbli S'un—Bill Eagle Feather—in his grave twenty-two years ago. Through his teaching and life example, he lives on. His spirit has made itself known to many over the past two decades, and not only metaphorically. In chapter 1, I told of how he appeared to me after his death and went to our house to visit Paula. His spirit went to see other people after his death, too; so they told me.

One of the things he let us know at that time was that after death a person makes a choice: he or she can choose either to walk the *c'anku wakan*—the sacred road to what might be called heaven—or to stick around and help the living in whatever way possible. I believe Uncle Bill took the latter choice, and his spirit stayed around, helping his relatives and continuing to be a good influence.

During the early rituals after we finished the log ceremony house here on our farm, before we had a lock on the door, we used to nail the door shut so nothing would interrupt us. In the darkness of the first ceremony many of us—Paula, Lyn, and others—saw the door open. Uncle Bill's figure was standing there briefly. It was as though he were blessing the event.

Shortly after this, Paula and I were sitting at the kitchen table, the same table at which Uncle Bill used to sit with us, telling stories and teaching us songs. We were talking about those good old times and how much we missed him. Suddenly, with a loud crash, a cookpot fell off the wall. We both jumped. It was as if he were letting us know he was still around!

But these ghostly manifestations gradually became more infrequent. In the end they make up only a small part of the greater influence he has had on our lives, and on the lives of many.

When Bill Eagle Feather opened up his world to us it took us to places we'd never imagined. For the first year or so it was like a honeymoon, new, wonderful, exciting. It was an honor just to be able to hear him, to be in his presence. The hard work came later, in following his teachings on how to make relations with the world, and particularly with people.

I came to understand just how great he was when I started passing on what I learned from him here at Eagle Voice Center. That's when I came face to face with understanding how difficult it is to be kind and patient with so many different people coming together. Only then did I realize how hard it had been for Uncle to establish and maintain Eagle Feather Culture Center at his place on the reservation.

A year or so before he died, Uncle Bill told me that he wanted me to make a teaching center here at the farm modeled after his. He wanted me to apply to the government for tax-exempt status, as he had. I wanted nothing to do with it and strenuously opposed his idea. He sent me a copy of the Sioux Nation Sun Dance articles and bylaws of incorporation anyhow and told me to write my own. I stuck it in a drawer and almost forgot it. But thirteen years later, in 1992, Eagle Voice Center gained federal approval. Uncle Bill was the one who started the ball rolling.

My conception of how things were going to be as a student was greatly at odds with my experience at the hands of Uncle Bill. I had read *Black Elk Speaks* and *Lame Deer* and other books. But doing is a lot different from reading. From my experience I would say that things are never the way we think they will be. Life is *never* what you conceive it to be!

I remember a young man who came to a Sweat Lodge ceremony here at the farm a few years ago. He had read many descriptions of the ritual and was eager to participate. When I talked to him about it he constantly interrupted with, "Yes, yes. I know, I know!" In the Lodge, as the hot rocks were being handed in, he began breathing rapidly. I whacked him on the head with my feathers and told him to stop hyperventilating. "I can't! I can't!" he cried, and bolted from the Lodge. He never came back. The actual ceremony overwhelmed him with fear.

In *A Separate Reality,* by Carlos Castaneda, the Yaqui *brujo* Don Juan tells Carlos, "Things don't change. We change our way of seeing." In our ignorance we believe that what we see is the true reality. Many people are shocked and disillusioned by some of the things medicine men say or do. Their disillusionment makes them blind, and they miss the essential power of the teaching. Many people saw Uncle Bill as a saint; but he wasn't a saint, he was a human being. The good and the not-so-good come equally in a man, and Bill Eagle Feather had plenty of both these qualities.

On the last day of the 1980 Sioux Nation Sun Dance, only two months before his death, Eagle Feather said something that shocked and disgusted many people. Over the public-address system, when the dance was finished, he announced to the singers and dancers and all present that after everybody left he was going to jerk the crotches that formed the sacred arbor out of the ground, sell them for firewood, take the money, and go get drunk with his friend Henry Crow Dog. Very few people understood how heavy was the burden of responsibility that he carried. They didn't know how disappointed he was that so many had failed to fulfill their vow by walking out of the Sun Dance before it was over (as I described in chapter 9).

Both Paula and I have had similar feelings many times in the past twenty years. The honeymoon is long since over; the sailing isn't as smooth as it was when we first began. Uncle Bill warned us that it would happen this way, but in our enthusiastic innocence back in the seventies we couldn't believe it.

Uncle Bill made Paula a sacred Pipe. He told her, "Hang onto this Pipe. Some day it may be the only thing you have to hang onto." She is still carrying it. For many years it was a heavy burden, which has become lighter in recent years as her understanding has grown.

Eagle Feather was a wonderful reader of people. In emulating him, I try to see the good in spite of the bad, the strength of a human in spite of his or her weaknesses. Both he and Henry Crow Dog wanted us to pass on their teachings. I try to tell stories in the way they did, particularly the way Uncle Bill did.

The result is that many people who come to Eagle Voice Center feel they are acquainted with Bill Eagle Feather even though they never met him. The big photo I have of him in the log house helps. Through his teaching he is an influence in the lives of many people he never met. The gift of his influence bears on people unknown to him. Even the young children of those who come here feel the blessing of his teaching. "Grandfather, your influence is in all these gifts."

All my Relations.

Bibliography

Brown, S. E. *The Sacred Pipe*. New York: Penguin Books, 1953.

Castaneda, Carlos. *The Teachings of Don Juan*. New York: Simon and Schuster, 1968 (twelfth printing).

———. *A Separate Reality*. New York: Simon and Schuster, 1971.

Fire Lame Deer, Archie, and Richard Erdoes. *Gift of Power: The Life and Teachings of a Lakota Medicine Man*. Santa Fe, N. Mex.: Bear & Company, 1994.

(Fire) Lame Deer, John, and Richard Erdoes, *Lame Deer, Seeker of Visions*. New York: Simon and Schuster, 1972.

Highwater, Jamake. *The Primal Mind*. New York: Harper and Row, 1981.

Mails, Thomas. *Sundancing at Rosebud and Pine Ridge*. Sioux Falls, S. Dak.: Center of Western Studies, Augustana College, 1978.

Neihardt, John. *Black Elk Speaks*. New York: Simon and Schuster, 1932.

Stolzman, William. *The Pipe and Christ*. Chamberlain, S. Dak.: Tipi Press, 1986.

BOOKS OF RELATED INTEREST

Gift of Power
The Life and Teachings of a Lakota Medicine Man
by Archie Fire Lame Deer and Richard Erdoes

Crying for a Dream
The World through Native American Eyes
by Richard Erdoes

Sun Dancing
A Spiritual Journey on the Red Road
by Michael Hull

Two Ravens
The Life and Teachings of a Spiritual Warrior
by Louis Two Ravens Irwin and Robert Liebert

Meditations with the Lakota
Prayers, Songs, and Stories of Healing and Harmony
by Paul Steinmetz

Call of the Great Spirit
The Shamanic Life and Teachings of Medicine Grizzly Bear
by Bobby Lake-Thom

Legends and Prophecies of the Quero Apache
Tales for Healing and Renewal
by Maria Yracébûrû

The Cherokee Full Circle
A Practical Guide to Ceremonies and Traditions
by J. T. Garrett, Ed.D., and Michael Tlanusta Garrett, Pd.D.

Inner Traditions • Bear & Company
P.O. Box 388
Rochester, VT 05767
1-800-246-8648
www.InnerTraditions.com

Or contact your local bookseller